Mario Tailgates NASCAR Style

Mario Tailgates
//// NASCAR® Style

By Mario Batali

PRINCIPAL PHOTOGRAPHY BY
Kelly Campbell

ART DIRECTION BY
Douglas Riccardi and Lisa Eaton

Book design: Douglas Riccardi and Lisa Eaton
Design production: Bob Parajon
Copy editor: Laura Wagner
Prepress manager: Russ Carr
Prepress specialists: Steve Romer, Pamela Speh

Food styling by Abigail Bodiker
Assistant photography by Thomas Mangieri

All photos by Kelly Campbell except pages as noted: (T= top; B= bottom; L= left; R= right)
Bob Leverone: front cover foreground and back cover, 6, 8T, 11, 14T, 19, 26, 32, 35, 46-47 (all), 50, 74, 84, 110, 131, 144, 156, 159, 162, 164-165 (all), 173, 186, 188, 190, 198, 199
Wilton Industries: 12, 13
David M. Nesi: 8BR, 38, 53, 55, 101, 122
Harold Hinson: front cover background, 22, 27, 36, 37, 79, 116, 121, 141, 152, 170, 171, 183, 205
Rusty Burroughs: 105
Bill Gutweiler: 108, 113
Erik Perel: 125
Karl Stolleis: 149

NASCAR Publishing
Senior Manager of Publishing: Jennifer White
Publishing Coordinator: Catherine McNeill

ISBN 10: 0-89204-846-8, ISBN 13: 978-0-8920-4846-5   10 9 8 7 6 5 4 3 2 1

Dedication

To Americans at leisure. We got it down.

Acknowledgements

Special thanks to:

My sons, Benno and Leo, who make every meal as fun as the Daytona 500.

Lisa Eaton, Douglas Riccardi, Kelly Campbell and Thomas Mangieri for making these thoughts look, feel and taste like a book.

Zach Allen and Abigail Bodiker for all of the food for all of the photos.

Viking Range for the cool mobile kitchen.

Chefs David Schnell and Herbert Word for showing us what great cooking from the South really is.

REM for such cool tunes that keep me cooking, even in the middle of a huge race.

The France family for allowing me into the party.

The Food Network for continuing to make food accessible.

My partners Rich Bodmer, Rich Adubato and Chris Adubato at Dyno Marketing for bringing me into the wild NASCAR world and helping me with the concept for this book.

CONTENTS

Most fans of sporting events slide into their seats at game time and leave as soon as the game is over or when the score is so lopsided all they can think about is beating the traffic. NASCAR fans are different. Usually they arrive days before a race and stay long after the checkered flag is waved. And that's just for a normal racing weekend. Fans who attend Speedweeks at Daytona can stick around for two weeks of events. That's a lot of racing.

And a lot of meals.

Because NASCAR fans do like to eat.

At Dover, I met a guy who proudly showed me the prime rib of beef he was roasting amongst the coals of his well-seasoned grill (one of the legs was dubiously propped up with a 2-by-4). It was clear from the excitement of his tailgating crew as they hovered around the grill that every year they looked forward to this rib as much as they did the race. Indeed, at Dover, I met many fans that had never sat in the grandstand, but instead stayed by their campers and watched the race on TV. And why did they bother coming to the track? For the spirit and camaraderie and, no doubt, the food.

Roaming through infields and camping areas at many tracks, spending time with all kinds of tailgaters, I quickly discovered there is no shortage of creativity and ingenuity when it comes to the typical NASCAR tailgating menu.

Basically, we NASCAR fans will eat anything. And we're proud of it.

Still, despite being omnivores, planning and executing three or more days of meals at the track is always a challenge. It's an even bigger challenge when you're cooking out of a miniscule camper kitchen or the backend of the family truck in a parking lot. In addition, there are the continual distractions of being among throngs of devoted fans eager to share with you the intensity of their exuberance.

Yet thousands of tailgating cooks rise to the occasion every week during racing season. Dinner is clearly the highlight. Lots of tailgaters have their special dishes, ones they can cook with their eyes closed. Neighbors who may have sampled some at the last race, will no doubt stop by in hopes of scoring some leftovers once again. But that's one of the great things about the NASCAR community. As one tailgater assured me,

"NASCAR fans always look out for each other. If one crew runs out of food, we'll feed them dinner that night, knowing they'll do the same for us, if not this race, then another time. It all works out."

You'll notice I've left lunch out of your tailgating responsibilities. I'm thinking your crew can figure out lunch by themselves. Leftovers or PB&J and a bag of chips should suffice. If you're feeling magnanimous, or you want to make up for the fact that you still haven't cleaned out the garage like you promised to last year, you can grill some hot dogs or burgers for lunch. Still, I think your time is better spent relaxing, so you're rested later when it's time to cook dinner.

I hope the simple, sturdy recipes in this book will give you ideas for new favorite dishes to both feed your crew and share among your neighbors.

I've also tried to anticipate most of the tailgating obstacles you'll face, the lapped cars you'll have to pass to keep up with the leaders. I hope using this book will make you feel like you have your own over-the-wall crew. That it'll get you dialed in with techniques, equipment, and tailgating info for all the tracks. It'll serve as your spotter, keeping you abreast of problems that might come up. Above all, I hope this book will provide you with sterling recipes to keep your tailgates, always and forever, on the lead lap.

Standing over the starting line at Pocono, holding the green flag as tightly as I could and watching the line of cars as they came out of the third turn and headed toward me down the backstretch, was one of the most exciting experiences I've ever had.

This book celebrates both a love of racing and of real food, of people eating together and participating in America's favorite pastime: watching and hearing and feeling the thrill and thunder of a NASCAR race.

Tailgating on the Inside Track

Equipment and Packing

Each week there seems to be some newfangled gadget designed to make a tailgater's life easier advertised on the tube. Usually, the reverse happens and you wonder why you asked for that portable blender for Christmas instead of the new set of wrenches.

While I could see tailgating with just a grill, tongs, and a few sheets of newspaper to cut the steaks on once they're cooked, I usually bring along a few more utensils than that. I might not pack my mezzaluna, but it's nice to have available some essential pieces of equipment I have come to rely on in the kitchen.

In terms of grilling, my tailgate menu planning mostly centers on my ample-size classic charcoal kettle grill and a carefully selected toolbox full of pans, bowls and utensils. If you have a gas grill, don't fret—I've addressed that in the recipe instructions. Unfortunately, you will need either a charcoal kettle grill or a smoker to prepare any of the smoked meat or chicken dishes.

TAILGATE TOOLBOX

Be super attentive to your packing list, both for equipment and ingredients. Once you're settled into your parking spot, there's no moving your camper until the race is over.

Every Tailgating Toolbox should contain the following:
- Long handled silicone basting brush
- Long handled grill tongs
- Long handled slotted spatula
- Grill cleaning brush
- Cast iron pan
- Several assorted prep bowls
- Several large spoons for stirring and serving
- Ladle
- Several serving platters
- 2 saucepans for reheating on the grill
- Chef's knife, serrated knife, paring knife
- Cutting board
- Plastic bags for clean up

For my absolute favorite stuff, please check out my kitchen tool line at www.italiankitchen.com.

GRILL

Many of the recipes included in this book require a portable grill. Gas or charcoal grills work equally well. You can cook food directly on the grill or, for dishes such as Old-fashioned Crab Cakes (page 69), you can use the grill's heat to cook in a skillet. After the meal, you can light cigars on the glowing coals.

TABLES

I always bring at least two: one for food prep, one for the buffet. Tables help define your space in the parking lot: the more you have, the more important and substantial your tailgate party must be. Also think about cloths if the tops of your tables are funky. You can get some with the number of your favorite driver. Or, if you're eating ribs, get some with the number of your least favorite driver because they're bound to get dirty.

CHAIRS

Chairs help. Your crew has a lot of important matters to discuss in the days or hours before a big race. Or at least they seem important at the time. The best folding chairs come with beer holders nestled into the arms—one on each side, in case you forget which hand you've been drinking with.

WATER

Always, always pack plenty of water, even if the track provides a potable water hookup. The temperature gets hot around the track. And if your kids are running around having fun, they may not realize just how hot it is.

KIDDIE POOL

The vast infield in Daytona is awash with kiddie pools, in which not just the rug rats are cooling off. Even Dad will take a dip. Lowering yourself into the pool and hoisting yourself out is sufficient exercise to justify having another burger.

Grilling Basics

Most tailgating food is cooked on the grill. So it's important you know the grill as well as the crew chief knows his car's engine.

Grilling is an art. It requires your attention. The grill does not do the cooking. You do the cooking. The grill merely gets hot. Just like a race track, conditions on the grill are never quite the same from one moment to the next. You have to feel out the hot spots on the grill and rotate the food to and from those areas. It's the only way to ensure that everything you're cooking will be done at the same time. Don't expect to throw a steak on the grill, catch a few laps at Happy Hour and come back to pull the steak off perfectly cooked. You must remain attentive.

Mastering the heat is really the only trick to successful grilling. Usually, I recommend a medium-hot fire or medium-high heat, if using a gas grill. When cooking thick pieces of meat, however, two levels of heat are better: a hotter area on which to sear the meat, a less-hot area on which to cook the center of the meat medium-rare. Medium heat is best for brats (see page 99) and hot dogs (see page 84) to help keep the skins from splitting.

Grilling tips

Do *not* forget the gas. Just because racing teams run out of gas sometimes and suffer the consequences doesn't mean you have to. Nothing is more humiliating than watching your flame sputter out just as the steaks hit the grill. (And no one makes a little blue pill to solve this particular problem.)

Refrigeration

If you inherited Grandpop's RV or found enough money to buy one, you likely have a refrigerator of some sort and can keep made-ahead dishes and leftovers stored until ready to serve.

Good quality ice-filled coolers can be substituted, although you might make an ice run or two, depending on your crew's tailgating endurance. (Most tracks have bags of ice available for a nominal fee.) Train your crew to shut the lid after digging around in the cooler for sodas. Pack and store meats and other perishable items toward the bottom of the cooler and, of course, keep the cooler away from direct sunlight. Ideally, pack one cooler of food and another with drinks to minimize the number of times the food cooler gets opened.

Be responsible and alert to food spoilage and safely discard any questionable food items. And remember, the cooler can't be too cold.

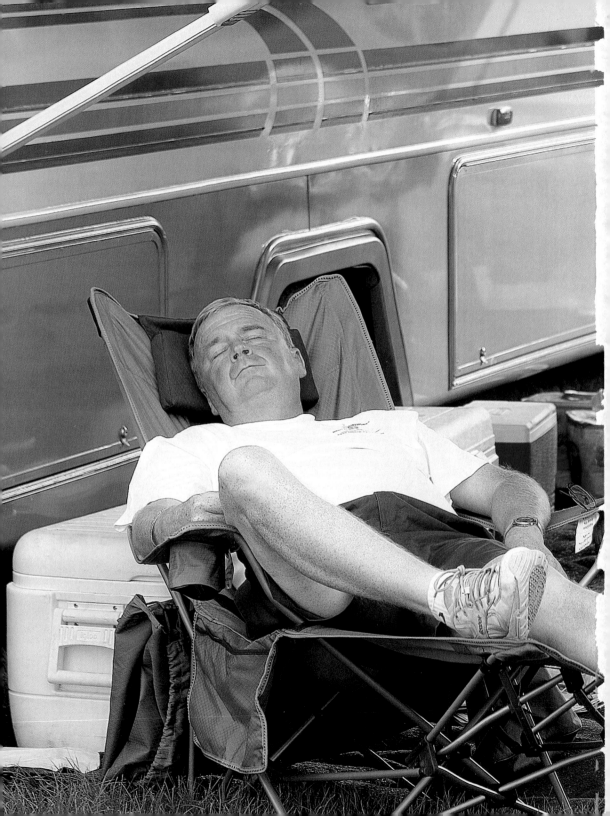

1
Breakfast

Morning happens.

At some point during the weekend, you have to wake up, most likely not at a time of your choosing. Maybe the kids from the RV next to yours are having a squirt gun fight—or maybe those are your kids.

Once your crew is awake, if not bright-eyed and bushy-tailed (squirt gunners excepted), everyone will most likely want to eat. And while the drivers are allowed a few parade laps before going full speed, cooks aren't allowed that luxury. Your crew is going to want some breakfast, and the shriveled brats you uncover on the grill from last night just won't cut it.

Here are some simple yet substantial breakfast recipes. They do require you to be awake enough to figure out which end of the knife to hold (it's the part that's not metal), but not much more than that.

Breakfast Tortilla Casserole

It's raceday morning and excitement is building. For the drivers, all the adjustments to their engines, transmissions, and chassis have been made. For the fans, all the adjustments to beer coolers, grills, and the level of the storage tank in the head have been made. Now it's time for everybody to enjoy a race-day breakfast.

SERVES 6 TO 8

2 tablespoons extra-virgin olive oil // 1 pound chorizo or other hot sausage, removed from casing and crumbled // 1 medium onion, finely chopped // 1 red bell pepper, cored, seeded, and finely chopped // 1 green bell pepper, cored, seeded, and finely chopped // 4 cloves garlic, finely chopped // 4-ounce can chopped green chiles // 1½ tablespoons chili powder // 1 tablespoon butter // 12 large eggs // 2 cups half-and-half // 2 cups grated sharp Cheddar cheese // ½ cup chopped scallions, green tops only // ¼ cup chopped fresh cilantro // 1 teaspoon hot red pepper sauce // 1 teaspoon salt // 16 ounces tortilla chips // Sour cream for garnish // Salsa Picante (see page 55) for garnish

1. Prepare enough coals for a medium-hot fire or set one side of a gas grill to medium-high.

2. Heat a skillet, preferably cast iron, on the grill. Add the olive oil and heat until just smoking.

3. Add the sausage and cook, stirring to break up the meat, until browned. Add the onion and bell pepper and cook, stirring, until they soften, about 4 minutes. Add the garlic, green chiles, and chili powder, and cook for 1 minute more. Remove from the heat and set aside.

4. Butter a 9-by-13-inch baking dish.

5. In a large bowl, whisk together the eggs and half-and-half along with the grated cheese, scallions, cilantro, hot sauce, and salt.

6. Spoon ½ of the sausage mixture into the bottom of the baking dish and top with ½ of the tortilla chips, breaking the chips into roughly 1-inch pieces. Repeat with the remaining sausage mixture and tortilla chips.

7. Pour the egg mixture into the pan and wiggle the pan a bit so the egg settles.

8. Wrap the entire baking dish in aluminum foil. Push the coals to one side of the coal grate. Place the baking dish on the opposite side of the grill rack from the coals. (If using a gas grill, place the baking dish on the side of the grill away from the heat.) Cover the grill and cook for about 40 minutes or until a knife inserted into the custard comes out clean.

9. Remove from heat and let cool for a few minutes before unwrapping. Be careful of escaping steam when you open the foil. Serve immediately.

NOTE: The sausage mixture can be made ahead. After it is cooked, let it cool, transfer to a resealable freezer bag, and keep cold in a refrigerator or ice-filled cooler until ready to use.

South of the Border Racing

Auto racing is making great inroads (literally) in Mexico. At this writing, racing is second only to soccer in popularity among Mexican fans. Ninety-four thousand fans turned out to see the first sanctioned NASCAR Busch Series race, the Mexico 200 held for the first time in 2005. What's even more impressive, and perhaps a better indicator of the potential racing has in Mexico, is the more than 38,000 people who showed up at the track for qualifying, close to a series record. The enthusiasm and wild excitement of the crowd during the race resembled the free-spirited feeling of the early days of racing.

The crowd rooted heavily for Adrian Fernandez—a homegrown driver who is now starting to make a name for himself in the world of NASCAR. Though a crash during qualifying had Fernandez starting in the back, he led twice before finishing tenth. The Mexico 200 road course took it out of the drivers, but Martin Truex took the checkered flag in what could become one of NASCAR's most historic races.

Sausage and Cheese Scrambler

After three days in the camper, it's likely your crew has made some adjustments regarding expectations for grooming and attire. This hearty breakfast takes this attitude into account. In other words, this dish may not look pretty, but it sure is tasty and, since you cook it all in one pan, it's a snap to prepare.

SERVES 6

12 large eggs, beaten // 1 cup grated sharp Cheddar cheese // 1/4 cup chopped fresh basil or 1 tablespoon dried // 1/2 teaspoon red pepper flakes // 3 tablespoons extra-virgin olive oil // 1 medium onion, thinly sliced // 1 red bell pepper, stemmed, seeded, and thinly sliced // 8 ounces white mushrooms, thinly sliced // 3/4 pound smoked sausage, cut into 1/2-inch slices

1. Prepare enough coals for a medium-hot fire or set a gas grill to medium-high.

2. Meanwhile, in a medium bowl, beat the eggs. Add the cheese, basil and red pepper flakes, stir to combine, and set aside.

3. Place a large skillet, preferably cast iron, on the grill over medium-high heat. Add the olive oil, onions, red bell pepper, and mushrooms and cook, stirring often, until the vegetables soften, about 6 minutes. Add the sausage slices and cook two minutes more.

4. Add the egg mixture and cook, stirring continuously, until the eggs are just cooked through.

5. Remove from heat and serve immediately.

NOTE: A 6-ounce can of mushrooms, drained and a 4-ounce jar of roasted peppers, drained, can be substituted for the fresh mushrooms and red bell pepper. One cup diced ham can also be substituted for the smoked sausage.

Eggs in Hell

These spicy guys will wake you up in more ways than one. The great thing about this dish is that it serves well at room temp, so there is no rushing around like a front tire-changer when the eggs are finished cooking. They can just sit on the table until everyone is ready to eat.

SERVES 4

4 tablespoons extra-virgin olive oil // 1 medium onion, coarsely chopped // 6 cloves garlic, thinly sliced // 4 jalapeño peppers, seeded and cut into 1/4-inch dice // 1 teaspoon hot chile flakes // 3 cups basic tomato sauce // 8 large eggs // 1/4 cup grated Parmigiano-Reggiano or Pecorino

1. Prepare enough coals for a medium-hot fire or set a gas grill to medium-high.

2. Heat a skillet, preferably cast iron, on the grill. Add the olive oil and heat until just smoking.

3. Add the chopped onion, garlic, jalapeño peppers and chile flakes and cook until the vegetables are softened and light brown, about 7 minutes.

4. Add the tomato sauce and bring to a boil. Immediately lower the heat until the mixture simmers and carefully crack the eggs one-by-one into the sauce.

5. Cook 5-6 minutes or until as set as desired. (I like the whites set but the yolks still quite runny.)

6. Remove from heat and sprinkle on the cheese.

7. Allow to cool 3-4 minutes before serving.

Pork Hash

Here's a great way to use up leftover cooked pork of any style.

SERVES 6

2 large unpeeled potatoes, washed // 6 strips bacon, cut into 1-inch pieces // 1 medium onion, finely chopped // 3 cups cooked pork, cut into small dice // 1/2 teaspoon dried thyme // 1/2 teaspoon salt // 1/2 teaspoon freshly ground black pepper

1. Prepare enough coals for a medium-hot fire or set a gas grill to medium-high.

2. Heat a large skillet, preferably cast iron, on the grill. Add 1/2 inch of water to the pan and grate the potatoes directly into the water. Cook, uncovered, until the water is gone.

3. Add the bacon pieces and cook stirring often, until cooked through. Add the onion and cook until softened, about 5 minutes.

4. Add the pork, thyme, salt and pepper and mix thoroughly, then press the mixture down firmly with a spatula. Cook until a crust forms, about 15 minutes. Turn and cook 15 minutes more, again pressing with a spatula.

5. Serve immediately with your favorite cooked eggs and manly hunks of bread.

NOTE: You can substitute the same amount of cooked lamb or beef for the pork.

Race day Morning

While you're sitting in your lawn chair, with your feet up, sipping coffee and eyeing one of last night's smoked pork chops resting on the grill and wondering if you have the nerve to eat it, the drivers are getting ready to race. Like most athletes, their morning before a competition is kept to a simple routine. Most have breakfast in their majestic motor coaches, the length of which would be the best run from scrimmage in most football games. This will probably be the last time they get a bit of peace and quiet until long after the race is over.

After breakfast, drivers usually appear at a meet-and-greet with some sponsors, where there is a lot of glad-handing and signing of autographs for the starry-eyed sons and daughters of sponsor VPs, not to mention the VPs themselves, who display the "Hot Passes" around their necks like Scout badges.

Late morning brings the drivers meeting, when the rules of the track are laid out. For many of the drivers, chapel follows. All this time, they are hydrating like crazy, knowing they'll be sweating like mad for the duration of the race. After chapel, the drivers mill around pit road, getting lots of hugs and kisses from loved ones and pats on the back from a whole slew of new best friends. After the driver introductions, the fly over, the opening prayer, and the singing of the national anthem introductions, the drivers head to their cars. When they hear the command to start their engines, race day morning is officially over and it's time for the drivers to do some driving.

Ham and Cheese Biscuits

One morning, I took a stroll through the infield at the Pocono Raceway with the charming and lovely Looie McNally, who runs the place. As we walked, an aproned woman appeared and presented us with a couple of these biscuit combos. They were wrapped in foil and still warm from the oven—nothing could have tasted better that morning! The generous woman disappeared into a camper before we got her name

You will need access to an oven to make this recipe. If your camper doesn't have one, you can make them at home and easily reheat them the next day at the track.

SERVES 8

2 cups all-purpose flour // 3 teaspoons baking powder // 1 teaspoon baking soda // 1 teaspoon salt // 1/4 cup cold butter (1/2 stick) // 1 cup less 2 tablespoons plain yogurt // 1/2 pound smoked ham, sliced medium thick // 4 ounces Cheddar cheese, sliced

1.   Preheat the oven to 450°F.

2.   In a medium bowl, whisk together the flour, baking powder, baking soda, and salt.

3.   Cut the butter into small pieces and add it to the flour mixture. Using your fingertips, rub the bits of butter together with some flour until they divide and are the size of split peas.

4.   Stir the yogurt into the flour/butter mixture until it just forms a ball. Knead briefly. It should be just the tiniest bit sticky.

5.   Transfer the dough to a cutting board or a clean work surface. Press the dough into a roughly 3/4-inch thick rectangle and cut into 2-inch rounds using a biscuit cutter or the top of a glass. Transfer the rounds to an un-greased baking sheet.

6.   Gently shape the remaining dough into another rectangle and cut some more rounds. Repeat to use all the dough.

7.   Bake on the center rack of the oven until the biscuits turn golden brown, 7 to 9 minutes.

8.   Let the biscuits cool for 10 minutes. If serving right away, cut each biscuit with a serrated knife and fill with a slice each of ham and cheese. Wrap in foil and let the lingering heat of the biscuits melt the cheese.

9.   If waiting to serve, let the biscuits cool completely, slice, fill with ham and cheese, and wrap in foil. Reheat them in a 350°F oven for 12 minutes, or on the grill over medium heat, and serve.

NOTE: You can use equal amounts of other combos of cheese and meat. One I like is prosciutto and sweet Gorgonzola. (You know you're a man if you have Gorgonzola in the morning.)

Green Eggs and Ham

The kids should love these if they're fans of Dr. Seuss (and who isn't?). These eggs are green from being topped with a Mexican salsa verde made with mild tomatillas.

SERVES 4

8 large eggs // ½ cup grated Pepper Jack or Monterey Jack cheese // 4-ounce can chopped green chiles // 1 pound center-sliced cooked ham // 1 tablespoon butter or vegetable oil // 10-ounce bottle salsa verde or tomatilla salsa // Sour cream for serving (optional)

1. Prepare enough coals for a medium-hot fire. When the coals are ready, arrange them so one side of the fire is hot and one side medium. Or, set a gas grill to medium-high on one side and medium-low on the other.

2. Meanwhile, beat the eggs in a bowl along with the cheese and chiles.

3. Grill the ham steak, turning once, until heated through, 6 to 8 minutes.

4. While the ham is cooking, place a skillet, preferably cast iron, on the hot part of the grill. Add the butter or oil and the egg mixture, stirring continuously until the eggs are cooked through.

5. Cut the ham into 4 pieces and serve with the eggs. Top each serving with a few tablespoons of salsa verde and a dollop of sour cream, if desired.

2
Appetizers

You may feel a bit put out having to assemble some appetizers, especially if you are in the middle of preparing dinner. But the fact is people have a tendency to get hungry before the main course is ready. They smell something sizzling over the charcoal, and they just have to eat.

To keep your crew from getting so ornery they grab the chicken off the grill before it's cooked—or the steak before it even makes it to the grill—it's best to have a few pre-meal bits and bites to offer them.

As lord and master of your grill, you will welcome any opportunity to display your grilling prowess.

You can always open a jar of salsa and a bag of chips, which I often do regardless. But the more cooking you do, the more leverage you have for skirting the less pleasant responsibilities of camper maintenance.

Remember, if you are using a charcoal grill to prepare some appetizers, you'll have to add more coals to the fire and allow them to come to full heat, before grilling the main course.

Shrimp and Hot Sausage Kabobs

Jeff Gordon's legendary crew, the Rainbow Warriors, was known for some of the fastest pit stops in the series. You can throw these kabobs together in almost the same amount of time.

SERVES 6

1 pound hot smoked sausage // 1 pound large shrimp (26-30 count size), shelled and deveined // 6 skewers for serving

1. Cut the sausage into ¾-inch slices, about the same thickness as the shrimp.
2. Thread the shrimp and sausage slices alternately on the skewers.
3. Grill the kabobs over medium-high heat for 5 minutes, turning once. Transfer the skewers to a platter and serve. If your crew is hungry enough, they'll figure out how to get the food off.

Drive for Show,
Pit for Dough

Fifteen years ago, there were no such things as pit stop coaches, video training, or pit practice sessions. Crews did their best each race, working off adrenaline and guts to get their drivers back on the track. While the technology of pit stops hasn't changed (gas can only flow so fast into the tank, after all), a new approach to training has decreased pit stop times during the last decade or so.

Like quarterbacks on Monday morning, pit crews study videos of themselves and look for ways to improve their times. Besides the obvious problems—"Joe, you changed the wrong tire—again"—they pick up on subtle mistakes that can hopefully be changed for the next race. Pit crews practice during the week, under the watchful eyes of their coaches, all in pursuit of cutting maybe a second off of their time.

Though drivers are always thanking their crews, fans caught up in the race often forget to watch the pit crews at work. I find their performance a fascinating choreography: part ballet, part defensive linemen running a stunt, and not unlike what happens on the line of a restaurant kitchen on a busy Saturday night.

Chicken Satay

If you like Thai food, then perhaps you've tried these fabulous skewers served with peanut sauce. They're a classic Thai specialty and well worth the few minutes it takes to prepare the peanut butter marinade.

SERVES 6 TO 8

¼ cup soy sauce // ¼ cup freshly squeezed orange juice (about 1 orange) // ¼ cup white wine // 2 tablespoons Thai fish sauce // 4 cloves garlic, finely chopped // 2 tablespoons freshly squeezed lime juice (1 lime) // 2 tablespoons finely chopped fresh ginger // 1 teaspoon ground cumin // 1 teaspoon ground coriander // 1 tablespoon natural peanut butter // 1 tablespoon packed brown sugar // 1 pound boneless, skinless chicken breasts, cut into ¾-inch strips // 6 to 8 skewers for serving

1.　In a medium bowl, mix together the soy sauce, orange juice, wine, fish sauce, garlic, lime juice, ginger, cumin, coriander, peanut butter, and brown sugar.

2.　Thread a strip of chicken onto a skewer, weaving the chicken strip back and forth several times so, the meat is not flopping and rests close to the stick.

3.　Place the skewers in a plastic container just big enough to hold them. Spoon or pour half of the marinade over the skewers, coating the meat on all sides. Keep cold in a refrigerator or ice-filled cooler at least 1 hour and up to 4 hours.

4.　Grill the chicken on medium-high heat, for 6 to 7 minutes, turning once, until it is just opaque in the middle and golden brown on both sides.

5.　Serve immediately with the reserved marinade as a dipping sauce.

Honey-glazed Ribs

Precook these ribs at home. A quick pit stop on the grill will have them heated through and nicely glazed, ready for your crew to dig in.

SERVES 6 TO 8

1/2 cup white wine // 1/2 cup soy sauce // 1 bunch scallions, green parts only, finely chopped // 2 tablespoons finely chopped fresh ginger // 8 cloves garlic, coarsely chopped // 6 tablespoons packed brown sugar // 1 tablespoon Chinese five-spice powder // 3 to 4 pounds babyback pork ribs (about 2 slabs)

FOR THE HONEY GLAZE

2/3 cup honey // 1/2 cup freshly squeezed orange juice (about 2 oranges) // 1/4 cup freshly squeezed lemon juice (about 2 lemons) // 3 tablespoons soy sauce // 2 tablespoons Dijon-style mustard // 1 tablespoon sesame oil // 1 teaspoon curry powder // 1 teaspoon dried ginger

1. Preheat the oven to 350°F.

2. In a large bowl, combine the wine, soy sauce, scallions, ginger, garlic, brown sugar, and five-spice powder.

3. Cut each rack into individual ribs and place them in the bowl with the wine mixture, tossing the ribs gently to cover with the mixture. Transfer the ribs and liquid to a large baking pan, cover with aluminum foil, and bake in the center of the oven for 1 hour. Remove from heat, let the ribs cool in their liquid, then transfer to resealable freezer bags and keep cold in a refrigerator or ice-filled cooler until ready to pack or for up to 2 days.

4. Just before grilling, in a small bowl combine the ingredients for the Honey Glaze.

5. Grill the ribs over medium-high heat, until they are heated through and nicely browned, about 15 minutes. Turn the ribs several times during grilling and baste them liberally with the glaze.

6. Serve immediately with lots of napkins.

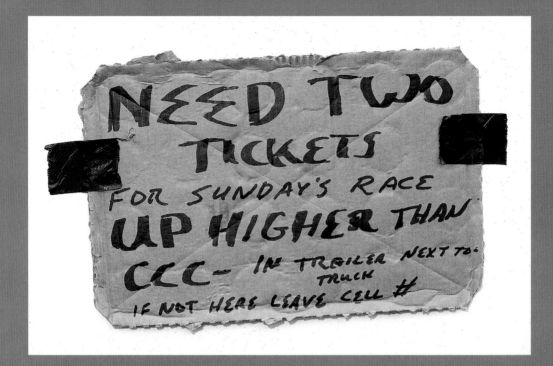

Talladega Boulevard

For many years, Talladega was the site of boisterous celebrations. Golf carts whizzed around, people hanging off the sides shouting words with far too many vowels.

These days, the infield at Talladega is a paradigm of NASCAR tailgating. The track is diligent about securing areas specifically designated for families. At Talladega, Mom, Dad, the kids, Grandma, and Aunt Bertha can park in a family friendly section and settle in for a weekend of racing fun. Toward the center of the infield is a place where the more exuberant fans can hang out.

While most of what earned Talladega Boulevard its rowdy reputation is now a thing of the past, you still might hear some exuberant whoops! during the night—part of the charm and uniqueness of NASCAR.

Spicy Chicken Wings
with Alabama White Barbecue Sauce

Talladega Superspeedway is in the heart of Alabama, where this unique sauce is popular. Talladega is the track that helped bring about the use of restrictor plates. Speeds are down now, but the long backstretch allows the cars to run wide open, and that's almost as fast as these wings will disappear.

SERVES 6 TO 8

FOR THE BARBECUE SAUCE

1 cup mayonnaise // ½ cup white vinegar // 2 tablespoons sugar // 1 tablespoon freshly squeezed lemon juice (1 lemon) // 1 teaspoon prepared horseradish // 1 teaspoon salt // 1 teaspoon black pepper

FOR THE RUB

2 tablespoons chili powder // 2 tablespoons paprika // 1 tablespoon garlic powder // 1 teaspoon salt // ½ teaspoon cayenne // ½ teaspoon ground cumin // ¼ teaspoon ground cloves // 3 tablespoons extra-virgin olive oil

24 chicken wings

1. In a medium bowl, combine all the ingredients for the barbecue sauce. Cover until ready to use or keep cold in a refrigerator or ice-filled cooler for up to 3 days.

2. In a small bowl, combine the dry ingredients. Rub the chicken wings with the olive oil, then liberally with the spice mixture. Transfer to a resealable freezer bag and keep cold in a refrigerator or ice-filled cooler until ready to use or for up to 4 hours.

3. Grill the wings over medium-high heat until the meat is no longer pink near the bone, about 18 minutes. You'll have to turn the wings a few times toward the end of the cooking to keep them from charring.

4. Serve the wings with a generous helping of Alabama White Barbecue Sauce.

Barbecued Wings Charlotte Style

North Carolina prides itself on its barbecue. Within a few miles of Lowe's Motor Speedway you can find any number of barbecue emporiums featuring their variation on this classic regional sauce. Of course getting in and out of the parking lot during race weekend is a near impossibility, so once you're parked at the speedway, you'll just have to make your own Carolina barbecue.

I like this recipe because you can precook the wings at home and finish them on the grill.

SERVES 6 TO 8

24 chicken wings // 2 cups apple cider vinegar // 3/4 cup tomato paste // 1/4 cup ketchup // 3 tablespoons packed brown sugar // 1 tablespoon peanut oil // 1 tablespoon Worcestershire sauce // 1 teaspoon red pepper flakes // 1 teaspoon salt

1. Put the chicken wings in a medium pot. Add the other ingredients and bring the liquid to a boil over medium-high heat. Immediately reduce the heat to medium-low and simmer the wings until just cooked through, about 25 minutes.

2. Let the wings rest in the pot with the sauce overnight in the refrigerator or an ice-filled cooler.

3. Grill the wings over medium-high heat until nicely browned, about 8 to 10 minutes. Turn the wings a few times during grilling and baste them liberally with the sauce from the pot.

4. Serve immediately with lots of napkins.

Queso Fundido

This Mexican cheese concoction is so intensely flavorful it'll quickly become your favorite fondue. Most likely, it will be your only fondue. If you don't have an official fondue pot sanctioned by the Society for the Prevention of Cruelty to Fondue, then you can just heat the mixture in a saucepan and set it out on the table. Reheat the mixture briefly when it gets too hard.

1 cup white wine // ½ pound mozzarella cheese, grated // ½ pound Monterey Jack cheese, grated // ½ pound goat cheese, crumbled // Two 4-ounce cans chopped green chiles // ¼ pound cooked chorizo, cut into ½-inch dice // 6 cloves garlic, peeled and thinly sliced // Salt and freshly ground black pepper // Tortilla ships for serving

1.   In a large saucepan over medium-high heat, bring the wine to a simmer. Immediately remove it from the heat, add the mozzarella cheese and Monterey Jack cheeses, and stir continuously until they are melted. You'll need to place it back on the grill for a few seconds to help it along. (If using a gas grill, reduce the heat to low for this step.)

2.   Stir in the goat cheese, green chiles, chorizo, and garlic. Continue heating and stirring for 5 minutes. Season to taste with salt and pepper.

3.   Transfer the mixture to a fondue pot and serve with tortilla chips.

NOTE: Let the mixture cool a bit before serving so your crew members don't burn their tongues.

Frittata Roll-ups

These curious appetizers are sure to delight your crew. Once you make the frittata crepes, get the kids involved rolling up the fillings inside.

SERVES 8

12 large eggs // 4 tablespoons extra-virgin olive oil // 1 cup prepared tuna salad // 4 ounces thinly sliced ham // 4 ounces thinly sliced Swiss cheese // 4 ounces sliced roasted turkey breast // 4 ounces thinly sliced Pepper Jack cheese // Tabasco or other hot sauce for serving

1. Crack the eggs into a large bowl and whisk until the eggs are well blended. Set aside.

2. Heat a 6-inch non-stick sauté pan over medium heat and drizzle with 1 teaspoon of the olive oil. Using a small ladle, spoon about 2 tablespoons of the egg mixture into the hot pan and swirl the pan, tipping the pan to get the egg as thin as possible (like a crepe), until it is just set and firm, about 45 seconds. Slide the egg frittata onto a plate and repeat to make 12 little frittatas.

3. Place 4 frittatas on a clean work surface. Spread a thin layer of tuna salad on each frittata and roll them tightly like cigars. Wrap tightly in plastic wrap.

4. Make 4 more roll-ups, using a slice each of ham and Swiss cheese. Then make 4 more, using turkey and Pepper Jack cheese. Wrap these up and keep all the roll-ups cold in a refrigerator or ice-filled cooler until ready to serve or up to 12 hours.

5. When ready to serve, remove the roll-ups from the plastic and cut them to resemble sushi rolls. Serve with Tabasco or other hot sauce on the side.

NOTE: Feel free to substitute your own fillings for the ones I've suggested.

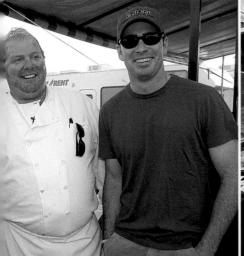

Prosciutto-wrapped Grilled Asparagus

Asparagus cooks at about 180 mph. Three or four minutes on a hot grill is about all you need. Let it cool a bit before wrapping the prosciutto around it. In fact, let the kids do that bit of assembly. Or, let your brother-in-law do some work for a change. You know, the one who somehow always wanders off just when it's time to clean up.

SERVES 6

2 pounds asparagus, medium to thick stalks (about 1/2 inch in diameter) // 2 tablespoons extra virgin olive oil // Salt // 1/2 pound prosciutto

1. Snap off the bottom of each asparagus stem, which should politely break right where the woody part ends. Using a vegetable peeler, peel the bottom 3 inches of each stem.

2. Brush the stems with olive oil and sprinkle with salt.

3. Grill the asparagus over medium-high heat until lightly browned all over, 3 to 4 minutes. (Be sure to place the stems across the grates so they won't fall into the fire.)

4. Let the asparagus cool, then, wrap a cluster of 3 or four asparagus in a slice of prosciutto.

5. Arrange on a platter, and serve.

Speedway Guacamole

Guacamole is one of those things people expect at a tailgate, like getting lost on the way back from a visit to the concession booths.

SERVES 6

2 ripe avocados // 2 tomatoes, seeded and cut into 1/2-inch dice // 1/4 cup chopped red onion // 1/4 cup chopped fresh cilantro // 1/4 cup freshly squeezed lime juice (2 to 3 limes), plus more if desired // 3 tablespoons finely chopped garlic // 1 teaspoon salt // Several dashes hot sauce // Tortilla chips for serving

1. Half each avocado lengthwise, remove the seed, and scoop the meat into a medium bowl. Mash the avocado with a potato masher or the back of a fork.
2. Add all the remaining ingredients and mix together well.
3. Serve immediately with the chips.

NOTE: If you make the guacamole in advance, place a section of plastic wrap directly over the surface of the guacamole, then cover the bowl and keep cold in a refrigerator or ice-filled cooler for up to 12 hours.

White Bean and Artichoke Dip

Tailgate enough and you'll probably run into some pretty wacky dip concoctions. I've encountered brave combinations—reputedly handed down for generations—such as beer and Roquefort cheese dip or pineapple-onion cheese balls, the consuming of which requires as much courage as passing while coming out of a turn at Darlington.

This dip is significantly safer and includes some of my favorite flavors. Serve with vegetables, pita bread, or crackers.

SERVES 6 TO 8

15-ounce can white beans, drained (liquid reserved) // 4-ounce jar artichoke hearts in oil // 1/4 cup extra-virgin olive oil // 1 clove garlic, coarsely chopped // 2 anchovies // 1/2 cup fresh basil leaves or 1 teaspoon dried // 1/4 cup fresh mint leaves or 1/2 teaspoon dried // 1/2 teaspoon salt

1. Combine all the ingredients in a blender or food processor fitted with the steel blade and pulse until smooth.

2. Serve immediately or keep cold in a refrigerator or ice-filled cooler up to 24 hours.

Smoked Salmon Dip

For a change of pace, try this fresh-tasting dip. Serve with vegetables, pita bread, or crackers.

8 ounces smoked salmon, finely chopped // 6 ounces cream cheese // 1/4 cup sour cream // 2 tablespoons finely chopped parsley // 2 tablespoons finely chopped scallions // Pinch cayenne

1. In a large bowl, cream together all the ingredients with a fork until smooth.

2. Serve immediately or keep cold in a refrigerator or ice-filled cooler for up to 24 hours.

Salsa Picante

The ideal appetizer. Set it out in a bowl and put a bag of chips next to it. Everyone knows the drill.

SERVES 6 TO 8

4 plum tomatoes, chopped // 1/2 cup canned corn packed in water, drained // 1/4 cup canned black beans, drained // 1/2 cup chopped red onion // 1 poblano pepper or red bell pepper, stemmed, seeded, and finely chopped // 3 scallions, green parts only, finely chopped // 1 tablespoon freshly squeezed lime juice (1 lime) // 2 teaspoons chili powder // 1 teaspoon dried cumin // 1 teaspoon salt // Dash of Tabasco or other favorite hot sauce

1. Place all the ingredients in a large bowl and mix together.

2. Serve immediately or keep cold in a refrigerator or ice-filled cooler in a sealed container for up to 24 hours.

NOTE: If you can't find any decent fresh tomatoes, you can substitute canned whole tomatoes drained of their juice.

Grilled Pizzas

You can buy pre-made raw dough at a pizzeria or a grocery store to make this recipe even faster and easier. If you decide to make the dough, keep in mind it needs to sit in the fridge overnight. As for the sauce, I love plain tomato puree with a little salt in it. But you can use store bought sauce if you like—just don't get too fancy. With good pizza, less stuff makes it easier and better (that maxim sounds more profound in Italian).

MAKES TWO 10-INCH PIZZAS

FOR THE DOUGH (skip this if you bought the dough)

1 packet dry active yeast // 1 tablespoon honey // 1½ cups warm water // 3¾ cups unbleached flour, plus ½ cup to work with // 2 tablespoons salt // 4 tablespoons extra-virgin olive oil, plus 4 tablespoons to work with

FOR THE TOPPING

¼ pound mozzarella cheese, grated // 2 cups tomato sauce // ¼ pound ham, sliced thin and pulled into pieces // 1 teaspoon dried oregano // 2 tablespoons grated Parmigiano-Reggiano or Parmesan cheese (optional)

1. **TO MAKE THE DOUGH:** In a large bowl, combine the yeast, honey, and water and stir until well mixed. Let the mixture rest until foamy, about 3 minutes.

2. Add the flour, salt, and 4 tablespoons of olive oil and stir until well mixed and the dough starts to pull away from the sides of the bowl. Turn out onto a floured cutting board or other clean work surface and knead until firm, 4 to 5 minutes. Form the dough into a ball, which should be about the size of a softball.

3. Coat the sides of a large, clean mixing bowl with 2 tablespoons olive oil. Place the ball of dough in the bowl. Cover with plastic wrap and set aside in a warm place, shielded from direct sunlight, until the dough doubles in size, about 1 hour. (This can happen quickly if it's hot out, so keep an eye on it.)

4. Punch the dough down with your fist so it deflates and divide it in half. Roll each half into a ball and place on a 11-by-17-inch greased baking sheet. Brush each dough ball with a little oil and cover carefully with plastic wrap. Keep cold in a refrigerator or ice-filled cooler overnight.

5. When you are ready to make your pizzas, prepare enough coals for a medium-hot fire or set a gas grill to medium-high. Arrange the coals so one side of the grill is hot and one side medium-hot, or, if using a gas grill, preheat one side hot and the other medium.

6. Line up the topping ingredients so you can easily get to them once you're at the grill.

7. Dust the work surface with a little flour and place one of the dough balls in the center. Press with your fingertips to create a thin, roughly 10-inch round flat crust. (If it is not perfectly round, do not worry. Also, this is not pizza dough that you can throw like in the movies.)

8. Carefully pick up the dough and place on the hot side of the grill and let it cook for 1 minute without touching it. If you move it before it sets, the results will be disastrous!

9. Using tongs, carefully loosen the dough from the grill and slide it to the warm side. Continue cooking until golden brown on the bottom and the top is just set and dryish looking, about 2 minutes more. Carefully flip the crust with tongs and put the uncooked side on the hot side of the grill and cook 1 minute more.

10. Again carefully slide the dough to the warm side of the grill and immediately place half of the grated mozzarella on it. Spoon dollops of tomato sauce over and around the cheese, reserving half of the tomato sauce. Do not worry about trying to cover the whole surface of the pizza.

11. Sprinkle the ham and oregano and grated cheese, if using, over the sauce.

12. Cover the grill and cook 2-3 minutes more, until the cheese is melted and the sauce is bubbling. Carefully remove the cooked pizza to a plate or board, cut into wedges, and serve (or, cover and keep warm while making the second pizza).

13. Repeat with remaining ball of dough and ingredients to make the second pizza.

Pork Scallopini Skewers

This dish has all of the flavors of my favorite Italian pork dishes but without the cleanup or tricky pan work. You can make it with lamb, veal, or boneless chicken breast or thighs as well.

SERVES 8

8 skewers for serving // Eight 2-ounce pieces of pork loin, pounded thin by the butcher (or you) // Salt and freshly ground black pepper // 1/4 cup butter (1/2 stick) cut into 8 pieces // 1/4 cup chopped parsley // 2 tablespoons capers // 1/4 cup grated Parmigiano-Reggiano or Parmesan cheese // 4 tablespoons extra-virgin olive oil // 1 lemon cut into 4 wedges

1. Put the skewers in cold water to soak.

2. Place the pork pieces on a clean work surface and liberally season each piece with salt and pepper. Put one piece of butter on each pork piece and sprinkle each portion as evenly as possible with parsley, a few capers, and a teaspoon of the grated cheese.

3. Roll each piece as tightly as possible to form a tube. Skewer 2 rolls lengthwise on 2 skewers to resemble 2 steps of a ladder.

4. Season the outside of each roll with salt and pepper and then brush with olive oil.

5. Grill all the skewers at once over a high heat until nicely charred on the outside, about 4 minutes. Turn and cook 4 minutes more.

6. Remove to a plate, sprinkle on the remaining cheese and let rest for about 3 minutes before serving.

7. Serve with lemon wedges on the side.

Mortadella Skewers

with Horseradish Dip

Mortadella is to deli bologna what Michelangelo's *David* is to lawn sculpture. It's so cherished in Bologna, Italy, that some of my favorite restaurants there have no problem serving a platter of mortadella before the start of an elegant meal.

SERVES 6 TO 8

1 pound mortadella, cut into 3/4-inch slices // 1 cup sour cream // 2 tablespoons grated onion // 1 tablespoon white prepared horseradish // 1 teaspoon Dijon-style mustard // 1/2 teaspoon salt // 6-inch skewers for serving // Kosher salt for serving

1. Cut the mortadella slices into roughly 3/4-inch squares.

2. In a medium bowl, mix together the sour cream, onion, prepared horseradish, mustard, and salt until well combined.

3. Fill a small serving bowl or pail, or empty beer mug, with Kosher salt to within 1 inch of the top.

4. Snag a mortadella square securely on the tip of a skewer. Invert the skewer and push the base into the salt, so it is secure and the mortadella is accessible. Repeat to make the remaining desired servings. The end result will remind you of a futuristic pincushion.

5. Serve with the horseradish sauce on the side.

Corn and Andouille Skillet Bread

Sometimes your tailgating crew might get a little feisty while they're waiting for dinner. If they've watched the *Smokey and the Bandit* DVD too many times and they've already memorized the names of all the crew chiefs, you might want to whip out some skillet bread that you made earlier in the day. Once they grab a piece, they'll calm right down.

SERVES 6

1 cup plus 2 tablespoons buttermilk // 1 large egg // 1 cup grated Cheddar cheese // 1/4 pound Andouille or other smoked sausage cut into 1/2-inch pieces // 6-ounce can corn, drained // 4-ounce can chopped green chiles // 1 1/4 cup all-purpose flour // 3/4 cup cornmeal // 2 tablespoons sugar // 1 teaspoon baking soda // 1 teaspoon baking powder // 5 tablespoons (1/2 stick plus 1 tablespoon) butter

1. Prepare enough coals for a medium-hot fire or set a gas grill to medium-high.

2. Meanwhile, in a large bowl, whisk the buttermilk and egg to combine. Add the grated cheese, sausage, corn kernels, and green chiles and stir to combine.

3. In a separate medium bowl, whisk the flour, cornmeal, sugar, baking soda, and baking powder to combine.

4. When the coals are hot, arrange them on one side of the grate. Hold the skillet over the grill to melt the butter, swirling the skillet to coat the sides. Pour the excess melted butter into the bowl with the buttermilk mixture.

5. Add the dry ingredients to the wet and stir just to mix. Transfer the mixture into the buttered skillet.

6. Place the skillet on the grill opposite the coals, or, if using a gas grill, on the side away from the heat. Cover the grill and cook for 10 minutes. Rotate the skillet so the opposite side is closest to the coals. Cover the grill and cook until the top of the skillet bread is golden brown and a toothpick inserted in the center comes out clean, 10 to 15 minutes more.

7. Remove from heat, cut into 12 pieces and serve. (Be gentle cutting the cornbread in the skillet as you don't want to scratch the bottom of the pan.)

NOTE: If you have an oven in your RV, or if your neighbors have one and they're off to enjoy Happy Hour, barter beer or other food products to borrow their kitchen and bake the skillet bread at 350°F for about 30 minutes.

Spicy Chicken and Cheddar Quesadillas

Quesadillas are one of the easiest appetizers to serve at a tailgate. Since you have to let the meat mixture cool before assembling them, it's best to make in advance, wrap them individually in foil, and then heat them up on the grill.

SERVES 8 TO 10

2 tablespoons vegetable oil // 1 pound ground chicken // 4-ounce can diced green chiles, drained // 3 garlic cloves, mashed // 1 chipotle pepper, coarsely chopped // 1 tablespoon chili powder // 1 teaspoon ground cumin // 1 teaspoon salt // ½ cup prepared salsa // 8 flour tortillas, quesadilla size // 2 cups grated Cheddar cheese

1. Prepare enough coals for a hot fire or set a gas grill to high.

2. Heat a skillet, preferably cast iron, on the grill. Add the oil and let it get hot. Add the chicken and cook, breaking up the meat into pieces, until it loses its pinkness.

3. Add the green chiles, garlic, chipotle, chili powder, cumin, and salt and cook, stirring, for 1 minute. Add the salsa and cook until the mixture thickens, about 5 minutes.

4. Transfer to a large bowl and let the mixture cool completely or keep cold in a refrigerator or ice-filled cooler for up to 2 days.

5. To assemble the quesadillas, put a tortilla in the center of a 16-inch-long piece of aluminum foil. Spread ⅛ of the cooled chicken mixture evenly over one side of the tortilla. Top with ⅛ of the cheese. Fold over the tortilla and wrap in a sheet of foil. Repeat with the remaining ingredients to make a total of 8 quesadillas.

6. Pack the wrapped quesadillas flat in a container and keep cold in a refrigerator or ice-filled cooler until ready to grill or for up to 12 hours.

7. To finish cooking, place the aluminum-wrapped quesadillas on the grill over medium heat and cook for 4 minutes. Turn them over and cook for 3 minutes more.

8. Remove the quesadillas from the foil and put each one directly on the grill and cook until they begin to get some grill marks, about 1 minute more.

9. Cut each quesadilla into 4 pieces (most easily done with scissors) and serve.

NOTE: You can replace the chicken with equal amounts sausage or leftover cooked steak, pork, hamburger, or fish.

Grilled Caponata

I serve a variation of this dish in all my Italian restaurants in New York. It's been a staple for more than a decade and is wonderful served with thin slices of Italian bread.

SERVES 6 TO 8

1 eggplant, peeled and cut into 1/2-inch slices // 1 large sweet onion, cut into 1/2-inch slices // 1 red bell pepper // 3/4 cup extra-virgin olive oil // 2 cups canned crushed tomatoes, plus more if needed // 10 Kalamata olives, pitted and chopped // 1/4 cup currants // 1/2 cup parsley leaves, chopped // 2 table-spoons chopped basil or 1 teaspoon dried // 1 tablespoon balsamic vinegar // 1 tablespoon capers // 1 teaspoon sugar // 1 teaspoon salt

1. Brush each slice of eggplant and onion with olive oil and grill the slices over medium heat, turning once, until golden brown on both sides, about 10 minutes. Transfer to a cutting board or clean work surface.

2. While the eggplant and onions are cooking, grill the red bell pepper until it is charred all over, about 10 minutes. Transfer the bell pepper to a small bowl, cover, and let rest for 10 minutes.

3. Chop the cooked eggplant and onion slices finely and transfer to a medium bowl.

4. Peel the charred skin from the bell pepper, core and seed it, and chop finely. Add it to the eggplant mixture.

5. Add the crushed tomatoes, olives, currants, parsley, basil, balsamic, capers, sugar, and salt and stir to combine.

6. Cook the mixture in a skillet, preferably cast iron, for 10 minutes over medium heat to thicken. Allow to cool to room temperature, or chill and serve cold.

Old-fashioned Crab Cakes

One of my favorite tracks is Dover, a.k.a. the Monster Mile. Its concrete surface and seriously banked turns make for some incredible racing—and Dover is in Delaware, which is crab country.

Which means there will be crab cakes.

Serve these before a simple entree. The minimal effort you put into the main course will pass unnoticed in the shadow of these delectable appetizers.

SERVES 4

FOR THE CRAB CAKE SAUCE

6 tablespoons mayonnaise // 2 teaspoons Old Bay seasoning // 3 teaspoons freshly squeezed lime juice (1 to 2 limes) // Several dashes hot sauce

1 pound canned lump crabmeat, picked over for cartilage and shells // 3 scallions, green parts only, finely chopped // 4 tablespoons finely chopped fresh parsley // 2 ounces Canadian bacon, finely chopped // 4 tablespoons mayonnaise // 1 large egg // 4 tablespoons plain breadcrumbs // 1½ teaspoons Old Bay seasoning // 1 teaspoon salt // Freshly ground black pepper // 2 tablespoons olive oil // Lime wedges for serving // Hot sauce for serving

1. To make the sauce: In a small bowl, mix together all the sauce ingredients until well combined. Cover and keep cold in a refrigerator or ice-filled cooler until ready to serve or for up to 48 hours.

2. In a medium bowl, gently mix together the crabmeat, scallions, parsley, bacon, mayonnaise, egg, breadcrumbs, Old Bay seasoning, salt and pepper, keeping the mixture as loose as possible.

3. Gently shape the crabmeat mixture into 8 roughly 1-inch thick by 2-inch in diameter crab cakes, handling the crabmeat as little as possible. Place the cakes on a plate leaving some space between them, cover with plastic, and keep cold in a refrigerator or ice-filled cooler for at least 1 hour or up to 4 hours.

4. Place a skillet on a medium-hot grill, add the olive oil and heat. Arrange the crab cakes in the pan so they aren't touching, and cook until they are nicely browned on the bottom, about 3 minutes. Turn the cakes over and cook about 3 minutes more.

5. Serve with a dollop of the sauce, a sprinkling of lime juice, and a few dashes of hot sauce.

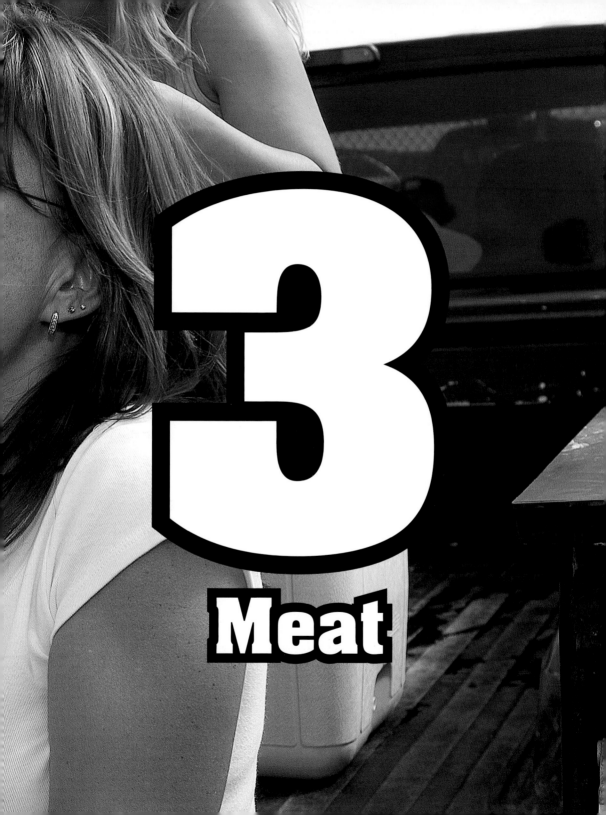

3
Meat

If the ghosts of Fireball Roberts or Tiny Lund happened to show up for a race, they might have a little trouble with the complex restraint system, but otherwise they'd be right at home. Because, once they were buckled in, they'd find three pedals, a gear shift, and a steering wheel.

Similarly steaks, burgers, and sausage have no doubt been part of NASCAR racing since the first checkered flag was waved.

What has changed a bit is some of the more adventurous seasonings and marinades that accompany a steak. By adventurous I don't mean ridiculous concoctions that you'll be looking to scrape off the steak without anyone noticing (even if you were the one doing the cooking). Everyone knows, grilled steaks and burgers taste great on their own; enhanced with some subtle yet potent flavors, they can be even better.

If it Ain't Broke...

Rusty Wallace is one of the best drivers in NASCAR history, and he's one of the most hands-on drivers in racing. For years, his tinkering and finessing have led him to more than 50 victories.

Rusty Wallace would not grill a good burger.

A good burger needs no tinkering or finessing or adjustment of any kind. Handle the meat as little as possible when you are shaping it into burgers. Put the burger on the hot grill and leave it. Don't pat it, don't maneuver it, don't try to adjust its downforce to give it more bite. Just let it cook, turn it over, and let it cook some more.

Caramba! Burgers

These spicy burgers are a change of pace from your regular, everyday burger.

MAKES 4 BURGERS

1½ pounds ground chuck // ¼ cup chopped scallions // 2 chipotle chiles in adobo sauce, finely chopped // 4-ounce can diced jalapeño chiles // 4-ounce can diced green chiles, drained // 1 tablespoon chili powder // Salt // 4 hamburger buns or 8 slices white bread // Salsa Picante (page 55) or prepared salsa for serving

I. Use your hands to combine the meat, scallions, chipotle and jalapeño chiles, diced green chiles, and chili powder in a large bowl. Shape the mixture into 4 patties about ³/₄-inch thick and 4 inches across.

2. Sprinkle the patties with salt and grill them over high heat for 4 minutes. Flip the patties and cook about 4 minutes more for medium-rare, 5 minutes more for medium.

3. Transfer each burger to a bun. Serve with salsa.

The Benno Burger

As soon as the first fans got wind of the races being run on the original beach course at Daytona, they must've arrived in their Woody station wagons, unloaded kids, a few chairs and a grill, and cooked up some burgers while watching Lee Petty duel Junior Johnson in the afternoon sun. This particular burger is named after my older son, who is in charge of the burgers at our house.

MAKES 4 BURGERS

1½ pounds ground chuck // Salt // 4 hamburger buns // Ketchup

I. Shape the meat into 4 patties about ³/₄-inch thick by 4 inches across.

2. Sprinkle the patties with salt and grill them over high heat for 4 minutes. Flip the patties and cook about 4 minutes more for medium-rare, 5 minutes more for medium.

3. Transfer each burger to a bun. Add ketchup. Serve.

Savory Roast Beef Sandwiches

There are all kinds of ways to gussie up a roast beef sandwich: Russian dressing, coleslaw, cranberry sauce. I like this one because it's just roast beef and bread, plus a hint of steak sauce, if you so desire.

SERVES 4 TO 6

FOR THE MARINADE

1 cup red wine // ¼ cup balsamic vinegar // 4 cloves garlic, finely chopped // 1 teaspoon dried rosemary // ¼ cup packed brown sugar // 1 tablespoon salt

2 to 3 pounds top round steak // 8 soft rolls or 16 slices white bread // Steak sauce for serving (optional)

1.	To make the marinade: In a medium bowl, mix together all the ingredients.

2.	Place the meat in a resealable freezer bag and pour in three fourths of the marinade, making sure to coat the meat on all sides. Keep cold in a refrigerator or ice-filled cooler for at least 4 hours and up to 24 hours. Reserve the remaining marinade.

3.	Remove the meat from the marinade and discard the marinade. Salt the meat and grill it over medium-low heat until it reaches 135°F on a meat thermometer for medium-rare, 14 to 16 minutes. Turn the meat several times to cook evenly and brush liberally with the reserved marinade during the last few minutes of cooking.

4.	Let the beef rest for 10 minutes, then cut it across the grain into very thin slices. Place a few slices of beef on a half roll.

5.	Rub a second piece of bread in any of the drippings and place it atop your sandwich and/or use some steak sauce.

Chili-rubbed Rib Eyes Fit for The King

It was the night before the race at the Dover International Speedway. I was cooking dinner for some of the drivers when none other but The King himself, Richard Petty, sidled over for some fixin's. He politely inquired if, instead of the *penne all'amatriciana* I was serving, he might be able to get a steak. Unfortunately, that evening there wasn't one around. But if he shows up again, I'll be ready.

SERVES 4

1 tablespoon extra-virgin olive oil // 1 tablespoon chili powder // 1 teaspoon ground cumin //
1 teaspoon freshly ground black pepper // Two 18-ounce rib eye steaks, cut 1 3/4-inches thick // Salt

1.   Prepare enough coals for a medium-hot fire, or set a gas grill to medium-hot.

2.   Meanwhile, combine the olive oil, chili powder, cumin, and ground pepper in a small bowl and rub the mixture on both sides of the steaks.

3.   Salt the steaks and grill them to desired doneness, turning once during cooking, 10 to 12 minutes for rare, 12 to 14 minutes for medium-rare.

4.   Let the steaks rest for 10 minutes. Cut them across the grain into roughly 1/2-inch slices, hide the ketchup, and serve.

Richard Petty at Dover

Richard Petty liked the Monster Mile. Between 1969 and 1992, he started 46 races at Dover and won seven of them, including the first two at the track and three of the first four. He also won two poles. Petty thrived at Dover because he was a master of taking care of his equipment and adapting to changes in the racetrack, still the biggest keys to winning today at the 1-mile concrete oval. Many feel Petty put NASCAR on the map. He helped to extend the sport's boundaries and established the standard for the close driver-fan interaction that continues today.

Thai Flank Steak

The sweet and spicy flavor of this steak always has me smiling. Oh, and I know you don't want to hear this, but often I'll grill an extra flank steak and serve it the next day for lunch, sliced thin over a salad.

SERVES 6

FOR THE MARINADE

1/4 cup chopped scallions // 6 cloves garlic, coarsely chopped // 2 tablespoons vegetable oil // 2 tablespoons Thai fish sauce // 2 tablespoons packed brown sugar // 1 tablespoon soy sauce // 1 tablespoon curry powder

FOR THE SPICY LIME SAUCE

1/3 cup freshly squeezed lime juice (about 3 limes) // 2 tablespoons Thai fish sauce // 1 tablespoon packed brown sugar // 1 scallion, finely chopped // 1 garlic clove, finely chopped // 1 teaspoon hot sauce

2 flank steaks, about 1 pound each // Salt

1. **TO MAKE THE MARINADE:** In a small bowl, mix together all the ingredients for the marinade.

2. Spread the marinade on both sides of each steak and wrap the meat in plastic. Keep cold in a refrigerator or ice-filled cooler for at least 4 hours and up to 24 hours.

3. **TO MAKE THE SPICY LIME SAUCE:** In a small bowl, combine all the ingredients for the Spicy Lime Sauce and set aside until ready to serve or keep cold in a refrigerator or ice-filled cooler for up to 48 hours. Let the sauce come to room temperature before serving.

4. Remove the meat from the marinade and discard the marinade. Salt the steaks and grill them over medium-high heat to desired doneness, turning once, 10 to 12 minutes for medium-rare, 12 to 14 minutes for medium.

5. Let the steaks rest for 10 minutes. Cut each steak across the grain on an angle into roughly 1/2-inch slices. Pour the lime sauce over the steaks and serve.

Thick Cut Thai-style Shell Steak

The dense coating of the vibrantly hot Thai chili paste used in this recipe starts off smoking. But don't worry, after some time on the grill, the heat mellows, and the flavor makes the steak just pop. Do not be afraid to give the steaks a copious spray of cooking oil before putting them on the grill. Cooking oil helps prevent marinades that contain sugar—as does this one—from sticking to the grill.

SERVES 4

1/2 cup Thai red chili sauce // 1/4 cup extra-virgin olive oil // 2 tablespoons red wine vinegar // Salt // 4 shell steaks cut 1 1/2-inches thick

1. Combine the chili sauce, olive oil, and vinegar in a medium bowl. Slather the mixture over the steaks and let the steaks rest in a refrigerator or ice-filled cooler for 4 hours or at room temperature for 1 hour.

2. Salt the steaks and grill them over medium-high heat to desired doneness, turning once, 9 minutes for medium-rare, 10 minutes for medium.

3. Let the steaks rest for 10 minutes before serving.

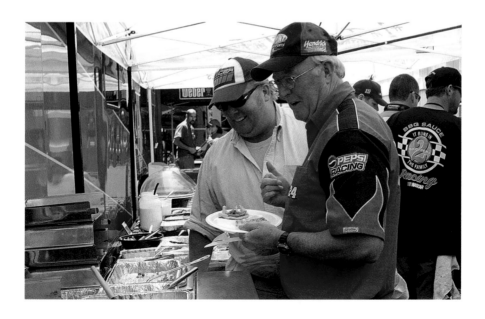

Coal-roasted Prime Rib

When Junior Johnson was working out the technique of drafting, it's likely a few drivers told him he was nuts—though they probably used a somewhat more colorful expression. But when his car, which, legend has it, was 22 mph slower, kept up with the field, people figured out Junior was on to something.

Cooking this whole rib roast might seem equally odd at first. You'll coat it with a thick layer of mustard and salt and then cook it literally in the coals on the bottom of the grill. Like drafting, the result is a marvel of physics and finesse.

SERVES 6

One 6- to 7-pound 3-rib beef roast, trimmed // 1 cup Dijon-style mustard // 2 cups coarse salt, like kosher salt, plus more as needed // Wire rack large enough to hold the roast

1.   Put the roast rib-side up on a clean work surface. Use a rubber spatula to evenly cover the rib side with the mustard. Liberally sprinkle salt over the mustard and press gently with your fingertips to form a crust. Carefully turn over the roast and place it on the wire rack. Continue the coating process so the entire roast is covered with a mustard/salt crust. Let the crust dry for 45 minutes, adding more mustard or salt as needed to keep the coating uniform.

2.   Prepare enough coals for a hot fire. When the coals are ready, using tongs, push them to the edges of the coal grate, creating space for the roast. Place the roast, rib-side down, right amongst the coals. Use the tongs to arrange the coals so they hug the roast.

3.   Cover the grill and cook for about 2³/₄ hours, adding more coals halfway through, or until a meat thermometer inserted in the thickest part of the roast registers 135°F for rare, 140°F for medium.

4.   Using oven mitts, carefully remove the meat from the grill. It's best to have someone standing close by with a large platter to hold the meat, as the outside of the roast will be very hot. Cover the roast with foil and let it rest for 10 minutes.

5.   Crack off the salt coating and discard, being careful as it will be very hot as well. Use a brush or paper towel to gently wipe any remaining salt or ash off of the roast. What you don't wipe away will just add to the great flavor.

6.   Carve the roast into thick slices. It's best to decide which three get the bones before you start hacking.

7.   Serve immediately, with the warning that anyone bellying up to the table who thinks they need something to go with this masterpiece can make it themselves.

NOTE: This recipe was designed with charcoal grills in mind. The flavors are dependent upon the technique of cooking the roast in the coals. Maybe you can borrow one in exchange for (a taste of) one of the ribs.

Salt and Steak

Making sure the camber of the tires suits the angle of the track is one of the adjustments an expert pit crew makes automatically. A minor variation can make all the difference in a race.

The same can be said of salting a steak before grilling it. Once the coals are hot, it's easy to get caught up in the thrill of the grill and forget one of the simplest and easiest grilling steps. But an unstinting sprinkling of coarse salt over the meat before grilling can make all the difference in the outcome. Timing matters: grill the salted side first, then sprinkle the second side with salt right away so you can be ready to turn the steaks when they are ready.

Hot Dogs Chicago Style

The Chicagoland Speedway is one of the newest in the series. It has taken a few years, but now there is more than one groove to the track, allowing for some serious side-by-side racing. In honor of the "dirty air" around a race car becoming an integral part of the Windy City's wind, here are some classic Chicago hot dogs.

SERVES 4 TO 8

8 Viennese beef hot dogs // 8 hot dog buns // Yellow mustard // Sweet relish // 1 cup chopped onions // 6-ounce jar sliced dill pickles // Chopped hot peppers // Celery salt

1. Toss the dogs in a large saucepan and add enough water to cover. Put the saucepan on the grill over medium-high heat and simmer the hot dogs until they are heated through, about 15 minutes.

2. Have the hot dog buns ready and line up the remaining ingredients on the serving table in the order listed. It's up to each person to develop a technique for getting everything situated in the bun.

3. When the hot dogs are cooked through, put one in a bun and hold it out. Repeat 7 times. I guarantee there will be a hand there to receive it.

NOTE: You notice there's no ketchup in the ingredients list. You can put some ketchup out on the table, but once you do, you can no longer rightfully call these Chicago Hot Dogs.

Barbecued Meatloaf

Once in a while, you gotta have some meatloaf to make you feel at home, even though you're parked with 40,000 other people. This meatloaf has hints of Tuscany, but you can still serve it with ketchup if you want.

SERVES 6

1/2 pound ground sirloin // 1/2 pound ground veal // 1/2 pound ground pork // 1 medium onion, finely chopped // 3 cloves garlic, finely chopped // 1/2 cup chopped sun-dried tomatoes packed in oil // 6-ounce jar roasted red peppers, drained and finely chopped // 1/2 cup plain breadcrumbs // 2 eggs, beaten // 3/4 cup milk // 1/4 cup freshly grated Parmigiano-Reggiano or Parmesan cheese // 1/4 cup chopped fresh basil // 1/4 cup chopped fresh parsley // 1 teaspoon dried oregano // 1 1/2 teaspoons salt // 1/2 teaspoon red pepper flakes

1.   Use your hands to just combine all the ingredients in a large bowl. Handle the ingredients as little as possible and try to keep them from being too closely packed. Transfer the mixture to a 9-by-5-inch loaf pan.

2.   Prepare enough coals for a medium-hot fire or set one side of a gas grill to medium-high. When the coals are ready, use tongs to arrange them on one side of the coal grate. Place the loaf pan on the grill rack opposite the coals. Cover the grill and cook for 30 minutes. Rotate the loaf pan so the other side is closer to the heat, and cook for 30 minutes more.

3.   If using a gas grill, place the pan on the side of the grill away from the fire.

4.   Transfer the cooked meatloaf to a clean work surface and let it cool for 10 minutes to set.

5.   Transfer the meatloaf onto a serving platter and slice.

NOTE: For a change of pace, or if you happen to have some leftover meatloaf, serve it cold or at room temperature. It also makes a great sandwich between some soft white bread.

Cheese Steaks Philly Style

Here it is: the classic sandwich from Philly. Have one for lunch. Have two for dinner. Besides cheese steaks and Pocono Raceway, Pennsylvania was once home to the Langhorne Speedway, where Grand National races were held from 1949 to 1957.

SERVES 6

2 pounds boneless rib eye or boneless eye of chuck in one piece, thinly sliced (see Note) // 1/4 cup extra-virgin olive oil // 1 large onion, thinly sliced // 1 red bell pepper, stemmed and seeded and cut into 1/2-inch strips // 1 pound white mushrooms, thinly sliced // 2 tablespoons Worcestershire sauce // 2 long French breads, each cut in thirds and then halved // 6 ounces sliced provolone or 6 ounces Cheez Whiz // 3 red or green pickled Italian cherry peppers, cut into 1/2-inch chunks

I. Have ready the thinly sliced rib eye.

2. Place a skillet, preferably cast iron, over medium-high heat. Add 2 tablespoons of the olive oil and the vegetables and cook, stirring frequently, until they soften, about 10 minutes (see Note). Add the Worcestershire and cook 1 minute more. Remove from heat and set aside to cool.

3. To make the cheese steaks, place a skillet, preferably cast iron, on the grill over medium-high heat. Add one third of the rib eye slices and cook, stirring continuously, until the meat is just cooked through. Add one third of the vegetables to the pan and stir and cook about 1 minute more.

4. Transfer the mixture to the insides of 2 of the pieces of bread. Immediately add to each 2 or 3 slices of provolone or a generous serving of Cheez Whiz. Top with a few pickled peppers—and you're golden.

5. Repeat twice more to make six sandwiches.

NOTE: Ideally, get your butcher to slice the meat and ask to have it sliced as thinly as salami. If you're slicing it yourself, put the meat in the freezer until it is firm but not frozen, about 1 hour. Cut across the grain with a sharp knife into the thinnest slices you can manage. Keep the meat cold in a refrigerator or ice-filled cooler until you're ready to cook it. You might find it easier to prepare the vegetables ahead of time, especially if you do not have access to a stove. Place them in a resealable plastic bag and keep in the refrigerator until ready to pack or up to 2 days. Let the vegetables come to room temperature before using.

Pocono Hangar Steak Fajitas

In honor of the Pocono Raceway, affectionately dubbed the Coat Hanger, I present these hangar steak fajitas.
SERVES 4

¼ cup extra-virgin olive oil // ¼ cup freshly squeezed lime juice (about 3 limes) // 4 cloves garlic, finely chopped // 1 tablespoon ground cumin // 1 tablespoon ground coriander // 2 hangar steaks, about 1 pound each // 1 red onion, thinly sliced // 1 red bell pepper, cored, seeded, and thinly sliced // ¼ cup chopped fresh cilantro // 1 tablespoon chili powder // 1 teaspoon salt // ½ lime plus its remaining half and 2 more limes cut into wedges for serving // 8 soft corn or flour tortillas for serving // 1 tablespoon hot sauce for serving

1. One hour before cooking, in a medium bowl, mix together the olive oil, lime juice, garlic, cumin, and coriander. Cover the steaks with the marinade and place in a covered container or resealable plastic bag. Marinate for 1 hour at room temperature.

2. Remove the meat from the marinade and discard the marinade. Grill the meat over medium-high heat until medium-rare, 8 to 9 minutes.

3. Transfer the meat to a cutting board and let rest for 7 minutes, then cut into thin slices.

4. Meanwhile, heat a skillet, preferably cast iron, over high heat for about 5 minutes. When the skillet is very hot, add the onion and bell pepper slices and let them sizzle for 1 minute. Add the meat slices, cilantro, chili powder, and salt and mix to blend the flavors.

5. Squeeze the lime half over the mixture. Transfer the fajita mixture to a large serving bowl and serve immediately with warm tortillas, hot sauce, and lime wedges.

NOTE: Remember to use a hot pad or oven mitt to hold the hot skillet when finishing the dish.

The Track That Ate the Heroes

As I was researching a little Pennsylvania NASCAR history, I came across the Langhorne Speedway, a.k.a. The Big Left Turn. It seems Langhorne was unique on the original Grand National circuit. It was, literally, a mile-long circle. No front stretch. No back stretch. Just, well, one continuous turn. In fact, if you found yourself going straight, you would probably wind up in trouble—and soon. Besides the monotony of the left turn, there were several damp spots from underground springs that fed onto the track, and a downhill-stretch just after the starting line, affectionately known as Puke Alley. The unique challenges of the Langhorne undid some of the sport's best drivers, earning it yet another nickname—The Track that Ate the Heroes.

OFFICIALLY LICENSED BY

NASCAR

Kansas City-style Beef Ribs

Long before it was home to the Kansas Speedway, Kansas City was known for its barbecue. And you can bet if a car hits the wall during a race at Kansas, there will be a bunch of guys in the grandstand thinking about how they could turn whatever's left of the car into a smoker.

SERVES 4

4 cups wood chips, preferably hickory or oak, or 12 to 16 hickory or other hardwood chunks, for grilling // 4 pounds beef short ribs // 1 cup favorite Kansas City barbecue sauce, plus more for serving

FOR THE MARINADE

2 cups pineapple juice // 1/4 cup Worcestershire sauce // 1 medium onion, thinly sliced // 2 tablespoons extra-virgin olive oil // 1/4 cup cider vinegar // 3 tablespoons sugar // 1 teaspoon mustard // 1/2 teaspoon salt

FOR THE RUB

2 tablespoons sweet paprika // 1 tablespoon packed brown sugar // 1 teaspoon garlic powder // 1 teaspoon ground pepper // 1/2 teaspoon salt

1. At least 1 hour before grilling, soak the wood chips in enough water to cover.
2. **TO MAKE THE MARINADE:** In a small bowl, combine all the ingredients and stir together.
3. Place the beef ribs in a resealable freezer bag and add the marinade, coating the ribs on all sides. Keep cold in a refrigerator or ice-filled cooler for at least 4 hours and up to 24 hours.
4. **TO MAKE THE RUB:** In a small bowl, combine all the ingredients and stir together. Set aside.
5. Remove the ribs from the marinade and discard the marinade. Pat the ribs dry with paper towels and sprinkle on an even coating of the rub, using your fingertips to press the rub gently into the ribs. Cover and set aside.
6. Prepare enough coals for a medium-hot fire. While the coals are heating, drain the wood chips. Use 12-inch square sheets of aluminum foil to make 4 packages of chips. Poke some holes in the top of each package to release the smoke during cooking.
7. Arrange the hot coals on one side of the coal grate in as compact a pile as possible. Place a packet of

chips directly on the coals. Place a 9-by-12-inch aluminum pan on the opposite side of the coal grate and add 1 inch of water to the pan.

8. Arrange the ribs on the grill rack opposite the coals. Cover the grill, with the vent positioned over the ribs, and smoke them until tender, about 1 1/2 hours. Add more wood chips every 30 minutes or so.

9. If using a smoker, follow the manufacturer's instructions.

10. Place a large sheet of foil on a clean work surface. Transfer the cooked ribs to the center of the foil. Pour on the barbecue sauce to evenly coat the ribs. Seal the ribs in the foil for 10 minutes to blend the flavors.

11. Unwrap and serve the ribs with more sauce ladled over.

Why Dry Rubs?

I used to think the drivers were testing out their steering when, during the parade laps before a race, they wiggled their cars from side to side. I now know it's a way of cleaning the tires, getting rocks and other stuff off them, and warming them up so they will better grip the surface. Since it's the tires that are in contact with the asphalt, it's critical they be as smooth as possible.

Hopefully, you don't have road grime in your pork chops, but you get the idea. The surface of the meat is in most direct contact with the heat and it must be appropriately treated. This is why I like to use a dry rub, either by itself, or in combination with a marinade. A dry rub adds a complex and richly flavorful crust to whatever you are grilling or smoking. Additionally, the rub will penetrate the meat, though not all the way, imparting a distinct, though more subtle, flavor not just to the surface, but to the inside as well.

Smoked Whole Rib Eye Roast

Say it's the weekend of a big race. And say, hypothetically, it's also the weekend of your wedding anniversary. Hmmm. One solution to this conundrum is not to say anything and hope your wife forgets. Another, more likely solution, is to do something really special, like making this exceptional roast. Serve it with one of those bottles of wine that has a cork instead of a screw top, and even when your wife informs you that your anniversary is actually next week, you will have yourself one memorable celebration.

SERVES 8 TO 10

4 cups wood chips, preferably hickory or oak, or 12 to 16 hickory or other hardwood chunks, for grilling // 1/4 cup extra-virgin olive oil // 6 garlic cloves, coarsely chopped // 1 tablespoon freshly ground black pepper // 1 tablespoon salt // 4- to 5-pound rib eye roast

1. At least 1 hour before grilling, soak the wood chips in enough water to cover.
2. In a medium bowl, mix together the olive oil, garlic, black pepper, and salt. Place the roast on a clean work surface and rub the olive oil mixture over the entire surface of the roast.
3. Prepare enough coals for a hot fire. While the coals are heating, drain the wood chips. Use 12-inch square sheets of aluminum foil to make 6 packages of chips. Poke some holes in the top of each package to release the smoke during cooking.
4. Arrange the hot coals on one side of the coal grate in as compact a pile as possible. Place a packet of chips directly on the coals. Place a 9-by-12-inch aluminum pan on the opposite side of the coal grate and add 1 inch of water to the pan.
5. Arrange the roast on the grill rack opposite the coals. Cover the grill, with the vent positioned over the roast.
6. Smoke the roast until a meat thermometer inserted in the thickest part of the roast registers 140°F for medium-rare, about 3 1/2 hours. Add more coals and another packet of chips every 30 minutes.
7. If using a smoker, follow the manufacturer's instructions.
8. Transfer the roast to a cutting board, cover with aluminum foil and let rest for 10 minutes before carving. Serve with some of the Argentine-inspired Tango Sauce (recipe follows).

Tango Sauce

MAKES ABOUT 1 CUP

1/2 cup extra-virgin olive oil // 2 tablespoons red wine vinegar // 2 tablespoons freshly squeezed lemon juice (1 lemon) // 2 garlic cloves, finely chopped // 1 cup fresh Italian parsley leaves // 1/2 cup fresh mint leaves // 1/2 cup fresh basil leaves // 1 teaspoon dried oregano // 1 teaspoon red pepper flakes // 1 teaspoon sugar // 1 teaspoon salt

1. Place all the ingredients in a blender or food processor fitted with the metal blade and pulse until just combined.

2. Serve immediately or transfer to a plastic container and keep cold in a refrigerator or ice-filled cooler until ready to use, or for up to 2 days.

HARDWOOD SOURCES

If you're having trouble locating hardwood to use for smoking, here are some sources:
(407) 382-3256, www.woodbridgechips.com
(800) 921-6808, www.bbqblanton.com
(888) 789-0650, www.barbecue-store.com

Brats

Brats are the universal tailgating food. I've found some version of them at every track I've visited. I've included them in the main course section, but I've known tailgaters to eat them for breakfast, lunch, and, at Bristol, when the race is run at night, as a midnight snack.

Brats must be cooked slowly over a medium fire—any hotter and the brats will burn and split and get ugly. Keep in mind that the average brat does not fit easily into the average-size hot dog roll, so keep your eye out for larger buns (no, I don't mean those buns).

SERVES 4

4 to 8 brats, depending on the usual brat consumption of your crew // 4 to 8 buns, depending on the number of brats you're grilling // Mustard

1. Grill the brats slowly over medium heat, turning them as needed to prevent charring, until they are nicely brown on the outside and juicy inside, 8 to 10 minutes. If using a charcoal grill, leave one area of the grill cool, so if there are any flare-ups you can move the brats to safety.

2. Serve each brat in a bun with mustard.

Sausage and Peppers

Here's a classic Italian dish, though it might be more popular in the States than in Italy. Since so much of the success of this meal depends on the quality of the sausage, it's worth investigating whether there is an Italian butcher shop in your area that makes its own sausages. Try a few of the flavors. Just keep tabs on which are hot sausages and which are sweet, so there won't be any unpleasant surprises.

SERVES 6

2 pounds Italian sausage, sweet and/or hot depending on your preference // 3 tablespoons extra-virgin olive oil // 2 red bell peppers, stemmed and seeded and cut into ½-inch strips // 1 green bell pepper, stemmed and seeded and cut into ½-inch strips // 1 yellow bell pepper, stemmed and seeded and cut into ½-inch strips // 1 medium onion, halved lengthwise and cut into thin slices // 1 small fennel bulb, trimmed, halved lengthwise, and cut into thin slices // Italian bread for serving (optional) // Red wine for serving (optional)

1.   Prepare enough coals for a medium-hot fire or set a gas grill to medium-high. Using tongs, arrange the coals so one side of the grill reaches medium and the other medium-hot heat.

2.   Arrange the sausages on the grill over the medium side. Cook, turning the sausages as each side browns, until they are cooked through, about 12 minutes.

3.   Meanwhile, place a skillet, preferably cast iron, on the medium-hot side of the grill. Add the olive oil and the peppers, onion, and fennel and cook, stirring frequently, until the vegetables soften, about 10 minutes.

4.   If using a gas grill, cook the vegetables first, over high heat, then reduce the heat to medium and cook the sausages.

5.   When the sausages are cooked through, add them to the skillet and cook for about 2 minutes more, stirring continuously to allow the peppers to absorb some of the sausage flavor.

6.   Remove from heat and serve immediately with some Italian bread and red wine, if desired.

Texas-style Smoked Babyback Ribs

NASCAR racing was first introduced in Texas in 1979, when, for three years, races were held at a track near Bryan. When the Texas Motor Speedway opened in 1997, Texas knew NASCAR was there to stay. It also meant Texas barbecue was officially introduced to racing. These ribs use a simple rub, but after a couple hours smoking in the grill, they emerge succulent and full of flavor.

SERVES 4

2 cups wood chips, preferably hickory or oak, or 6 to 8 hickory or other hardwood chunks, for grilling // 1/4 cup paprika // 3 tablespoons packed brown sugar // 2 tablespoons salt // 1 teaspoon garlic powder // 1/2 teaspoon ground cumin // 2 racks babyback ribs // 2 cups Mario's Kick-ass Barbecue Sauce (page 127)

1. One hour before grilling, soak the wood chips in enough water to cover.

2. In a small bowl, mix together the paprika, brown sugar, salt, garlic powder, and cumin. Place the racks on a clean work surface and rub the garlic mixture into both sides of the ribs. Let rest for 2 hours at room temperature or wrap in plastic and keep cold in a refrigerator or ice-filled cooler for up to 24 hours.

3. Prepare enough coals for a hot fire. While the coals are heating, drain the wood chips. Use 12-inch square sheets of aluminum foil to make 3 packages of chips. Poke some holes in the top of each package to release the smoke during cooking.

4. Arrange the hot coals on one side of the coal grate in as compact a pile as possible. Place a 9-by-12-inch aluminum pan on the opposite side of the grate and add 1 inch of water. Place a packet of chips directly on the coals.

5. Arrange the racks of ribs on the grill rack above the drip pan. Cover the grill, with the vent positioned over the ribs.

6. Smoke the ribs for about 2 hours, adding more coals and another packet of chips about every 30 minutes. After the first hour of cooking, swap the position of the racks of ribs so the one closer to the coals is on the outside edge.

7. If using a gas grill or smoker, follow the manufacturer's instructions.

8. Transfer the racks to a cutting board and cut them into individual ribs. Serve with some of Mario's Kick-ass Barbecue Sauce (page 127) or, if you're pressed for time, you can substitute some **2 BROTHERS** Barbecue Sauce. You can do that, on occasion, even if you're not pressed for time.

Bacon-wrapped Pork Kabobs

The smoky flavor of the bacon makes this dish a killer!

SERVES 6

FOR THE RUB

1 tablespoon paprika // 1 tablespoon chili powder // 1 teaspoon garlic powder // 1 teaspoon sugar //
1 teaspoon freshly ground black pepper

2 pork tenderloins, about 1 pound each, cut into 1-inch pieces // 12 slices smoked bacon, thickly cut,
then halved // Twelve 12-inch skewers soaked in water for 1 hour, for serving

FOR THE MARINADE

1/2 cup Dijon-style mustard // 2 tablespoons honey // 1 tablespoon Worcestershire sauce //
1 teaspoon dried thyme // 1 teaspoon dried rosemary // 1 teaspoon hot sauce

I. In a large bowl, mix together the ingredients for the rub. Add the pork pieces and toss gently to coat.

2. Wrap a half-slice of bacon around a piece of the pork and thread onto a skewer. Leaving a bit of room
between each piece, continue until all the pieces of pork are skewered. Arrange the skewers on a large
platter and set aside.

3. In a medium bowl, mix together the ingredients for the marinade and pour it over the kabobs. Cover
and marinate in the refrigerator for 1 hour or up to 4 hours.

4. Prepare enough coals for a medium fire or set a gas grill to medium. Grill the kabobs over medium
heat until they are just cooked through, about 12 minutes.

5. Remove from heat and serve immediately.

Pork Chops

with Cherry Barbecue Sauce

It's only natural that racing would find its way to Michigan, birthplace of America's auto industry. Cale Yarborough won the first premier NASCAR race at Michigan International Speedway in 1969. Michigan is known for its abundant cherry crop, hence this sweet and tangy cherry barbecue sauce.

SERVES 4

2 tablespoons packed brown sugar // 2 tablespoons extra-virgin olive oil // 1/4 cup freshly squeezed orange juice (about 1 orange) // 2 teaspoons chili powder // 1 teaspoon cumin // 4 boneless pork loin chops, cut 1 inch thick

1.   In a small bowl, combine all the ingredients except the pork chops and stir together.

2.   Place the pork chops in a resealable freezer bag and pour in the marinade, making sure to coat the meat on all sides. Keep cold in a refrigerator or ice-filled cooler for at least 4 hours and up to 24 hours.

3.   Prepare enough coals for a medium-hot fire or set a gas grill to medium. Remove the chops from the marinade and discard the marinade.

4.   Grill the chops over medium heat for about 12 minutes, turning once midway through the cooking. (I like them when they're still a tiny bit pink in the center, but that's up to you.)

5.   Remove from heat and serve immediately with the Cherry Barbecue Sauce.

Cherry Barbecue Sauce
MAKES ABOUT 3 CUPS

1 medium onion // 3 garlic cloves // 1 tablespoon chili powder // 2 cups canned crushed tomatoes // 1/2 cup freshly squeezed orange juice, about 2 oranges) // 1/2 cup ketchup // 1/4 cup packed brown sugar // 1 cup frozen sweet cherries

1.   In a medium saucepan, cook the onion over medium-high heat, until it softens, about 8 minutes. Add the garlic and chili powder and cook 1 minute more. Add the tomatoes, orange juice, ketchup, sugar, and cherries and cook 5 minutes more, stirring frequently.

2.   Transfer the mixture to a blender or a food processor fitted with the metal blade and blend until smooth. Transfer to a plastic container and keep cold in a refrigerator or ice-filled cooler until ready to use or for up to one week.

Hot Subs Molto Style

I make these special subs for my kids on a race weekend when we are in New York City. No reason you can't do the same.

SERVES 4

4 fresh sub rolls // 6 ounces capicola ham, sliced thin // 6 ounces genoa salami, sliced thin // 6 ounces provolone cheese, sliced thin // 6 ounces prosciutto, sliced thin // 6-ounce jar roasted red peppers, drained and cut into 1-inch strips // 1 cup chopped cherry peppers // 4 ounces good quality grain mustard // ¼ cup relish

1.   Working on a clean work surface, on each sub roll assemble the capicola, salami, provolone, prosciutto, roasted red pepper, chopped cherry peppers, relish and mustard.

2.   Wrap the assembled sandwiches in aluminum foil and place them on a grill over a medium-hot fire or on a gas grill set to medium-high. Put a heat-proof weight on each sub—a brick from your high school works fine. Heat for 5 minutes, turn the subs over, heat 5 minutes more.

3.   Remove from heat and serve immediately.

NOTE: For a stress-free dinner, assemble the subs in the morning, wrap in foil, and keep cold in a refrigerator or ice-filled cooler until you're ready to grill.

When in Rome

I always make it a point to give the chef, me, an occasional meal off. So doing makes me happy and ensures that I'll have the energy and enthusiasm to cook the rest of the meals. What it also does is give me an opportunity to sample some of the local fare each track has to offer.

Here are some I recommend trying:

- Chili dogs at Martinsville Speedway
- Smoked turkey leg at Atlanta Motor Speedway
- Pulled pork at Bristol Motor Speedway
- Brisket sandwich at Texas Motor Speedway
- Smoked sausage at Lowe's Motor Speedway
- Corn dogs at Indianapolis Motor Speedway

Skirt Steak Asada Tacos

This is the classic Mexican preparation that makes the most incredible tacos. These are assembled the traditional way, with just the meat, some chopped onion and cilantro, and a sprinkling of fresh lime. Once you get used to this kind of purity, you'll have a hard time dealing with what usually passes for a taco.

SERVES 4

2 tablespoons extra-virgin olive oil // 1 medium yellow onion, coarsely chopped // 2 medium poblano peppers, cored, seeded, and cut into thin strips // 4 cloves garlic, coarsely chopped // 1 tablespoon chili powder // 1 teaspoon ground cumin // 6 canned plum tomatoes, drained // 1 teaspoon salt, plus more for grilling // 2 pounds skirt steak // 1 medium red onion, finely chopped // 1 bunch chopped cilantro to yield 1 cup // 1/4 cup freshly squeezed lime juice (2 to 3 limes) // 8 soft corn tortillas // 3 limes cut into wedges for serving

I. At home, place a skillet, preferably cast iron, over medium-high heat. Add the olive oil and when it gets hot, add the yellow onion and pepper and cook until they soften, about 8 minutes. Add the garlic, chili powder, and cumin and cook 1 minute more. Add the plum tomatoes and salt, reduce the heat to medium-low, and cook 5 minutes more.

2. Transfer the mixture to a blender or food processor fitted with the metal blade and pulse until just smooth.

3. Place the skirt steaks in a resealable plastic freezer bag and add half the puree, making sure they are completely coated. Keep refrigerated or in a cold ice chest for up to 72 hours.

4. When you're ready to grill them, salt the steaks and grill them over medium-high heat, turning once, until they are a deep, rich brown on both sides, about 9 minutes. Transfer the steaks to a cutting board and let rest.

5. Meanwhile, in a medium bowl mix together the chopped red onion, cilantro, and lime juice.

6. Cut the steaks into 1/2-inch slices. Put a few slices in a warmed tortilla and add a heaping tablespoon of the onion/cilantro mixture. Squeeze some lime over the meat and then a tablespoon of the pureed sauce. Repeat to make 8 tacos.

7. Eat, and smile.

Smoked Pork Chops

I like to serve these with some sauerkraut and spicy brown mustard.

SERVES 4

FOR THE RUB

2 tablespoons packed brown sugar // 1 teaspoon paprika // 1 teaspoon salt // 1 teaspoon caraway seeds // ½ teaspoon ground allspice // ½ teaspoon freshly ground black pepper

2 cups wood chips, preferably hickory or oak, or 6 to 8 hickory or other hardwood chunks, for grilling // 2 tablespoons cider vinegar // 4 pork loin chops, cut 1½ inches thick // 1 pound sauerkraut for serving // Brown mustard for serving

1. At least 1 hour before grilling, soak the wood chips in enough water to cover.
2. **TO MAKE THE RUB:** In a small bowl, mix together the ingredients for the rub.
3. Place the chops on a clean work surface. Brush the chops with vinegar and then press the spice rub on both sides. Let the chops rest for 1 hour at room temperature or wrap in plastic and keep cold in a refrigerator or ice-filled cooler for up to 12 hours.
4. Prepare enough coals for a hot fire. While the coals are heating, drain the wood chips. Use 12-inch square sheets of aluminum foil to make 3 packages of chips. Poke some holes in the top of each package to release the smoke during cooking.
5. Arrange the hot coals on one side of the grill in as compact a pile as possible. Place a 9-by-12-inch aluminum pan on the opposite side of the grill bottom and add 1 inch of water. Place a packet of chips directly on the coals. Place the chops on the grill rack opposite the coals. Cover the grill with the vent positioned over the chops.
6. Smoke the chops until they are just slightly pink in the center, about 1¾ hours. Add more coals and another packet of chips about every 30 minutes.
7. If using a smoker, follow the manufacturer's instructions.
8. Remove from heat and serve with the sauerkraut and mustard.

St. Louis–style Pork Tenderloins

St. Louis is a NASCAR town. Gateway International Raceway hosts both NASCAR Busch Series and NASCAR CRAFTSMAN Truck Series races and it's the hometown of Mike, Kenny and Rusty Wallace. St. Louis is also home to the distinctive sweet-and-sour flavor of this sauce, which goes particularly well with grilled pork. Brining the pork in salt and sugar makes it come off the grill juicier and with denser flavor.

SERVES 6

½ cup kosher salt // ½ cup sugar // 2 pork tenderloins, about 1 pound each // 1 cup water // 1 cup ketchup // ⅓ cup cider vinegar // ⅓ cup Worcestershire sauce // ¼ cup packed brown sugar // ¼ cup maple syrup // 1 teaspoon hot sauce // 1 teaspoon salt // 1 teaspoon chili powder // 1 teaspoon Dijon mustard // 1 teaspoon celery seeds // 1 teaspoon paprika

1. In a large bowl half full of cold water, dissolve the salt and sugar. Put the pork tenderloins in the bowl and let them brine in the refrigerator or ice chest for at least 1 hour and up to 4 hours. Remove the loins from the brine, rinse well, and pat them dry.

2. In a medium bowl mix together the remaining ingredients until combined and set aside until ready to use.

3. Grill the tenderloins over medium-high heat for 16 minutes, turning and basting with the sauce every few minutes.

4. Transfer to a cutting board and let the loins rest for 5 minutes. Slice the loins on an angle and serve with the remaining sauce.

Grilled Tequila and Chipotle-rubbed Lamb

The road courses at Watkins Glen and Sonoma offer a challenging change of pace for many race car drivers. They get to turn right. They get to shift gears constantly. There are no banked curves. This lamb offers a change of pace from the classic grilled steak.

It is best to start this marinating at home and grill when you get to the track.

SERVES 6 TO 8

2 tablespoons vegetable oil // 1 medium onion, coarsely chopped // 7 garlic cloves, coarsely chopped // 1 cup jarred green tomatilla salsa // 1/4 cup tequila // 2 chipotle chiles in adobo sauce, finely chopped // 1 teaspoon chili powder // 1 teaspoon sugar // 1 teaspoon kosher salt, plus more for grilling // 1/2 teaspoon cinnamon

1 leg of lamb (6 to 7 pounds), boned, butterflied, fat trimmed and cut to an even thickness of 2 to 2 1/2 inches

1. Place a skillet, preferably cast iron, over medium heat. Add the oil and let it get hot. Add the onion and cook, stirring often, until it softens, about 8 minutes. Add the garlic and cook 1 minute more. Add the tomatilla salsa, tequila, chipotle chiles, chili powder, sugar, salt, and cinnamon and stir together.

2. Increase heat to medium-high and cook 4 minutes more, stirring often, to burn off the alcohol and thicken the sauce.

3. Transfer the mixture to a blender or a food processor fitted with the metal blade and pulse until just smooth. Let cool.

4. Place the lamb on a clean work surface. Spread the tequila/chipotle mixture completely over the meat. Cover and refrigerate to marinate at least 2 hours or for up to 48 hours. Allow the lamb to come to room temperature before cooking.

5. Grill over medium-high heat, turning once for medium-rare, about 24 minutes (a meat thermometer inserted at the thickest part should register 140°F).

6. Remove from heat and let the lamb rest for 10 minutes under an aluminum foil tent, then slice.

NOTE: The center portion of the butterflied leg is usually thinner than the two end sections. I like to trim that off when it is medium rare and let the thicker end sections cook about 5 minutes longer.

4

Chicken and (DON'T SAY IT TOO LOUDLY) Fish

Yes, just about everyone loves a steak or burger. But having some other dinner options can definitely come in handy, like having a few extra gallons of gas hidden in your roll bar.

Because once in a while, your crew might want something for dinner other than a grilled rib eye or barbecued pork.

Before you retire them to the garage to be stripped for parts, consider making a few of these recipes. Trust me, this is some good food.

Chicken is a natural for the grill. Remember that white meat cooks faster than dark. If you combine the two on the grill, remove the breasts a few minutes ahead of legs and thighs.

Fish also tastes great fresh from the grill. Unless you have a wood-burning pizza oven in which to roast a whole fish at 700°F, then grilling is the way to go. Fish does cook quickly, but don't be afraid to give it a good stay over the coals. I like fish best when it's slightly charred and has picked up some flavor from the coals.

Cuban-style Chicken Thighs

with Grapefruit Mojo

This Cuban-inspired chicken dish is killer on hot race-day evenings—perfect for Homestead-Miami Speedway.

Mojo is like a Cuban vinaigrette—there are many variations and it accompanies just about anything. To save time, prepare it at home and have it ready to serve once you've grilled the chicken.

SERVES 4

FOR THE MARINADE

1 medium onion, coarsely chopped // 1 cup fresh cilantro leaves // 4 scallions, green parts only, coarsely chopped // 8 cloves garlic, coarsely chopped // 1½ cups freshly squeezed orange juice (about 6 oranges) // ½ cup freshly squeezed lime juice (about 4 limes) // 2 tablespoons soy sauce // 1 tablespoon hot sauce // 1 teaspoon salt // 1 teaspoon ground cumin

12 chicken thighs

1.	Put all the ingredients for the marinade in a blender or food processor fitted with the metal blade and puree until just smooth.

2.	Place the chicken thighs in a resealable freezer bag. Pour in half the marinade, making sure the thighs are coated on all sides and chill in a refrigerator or ice-filled cooler for at least 1 hour and up to 4, but no longer. Reserve the remaining marinade.

3.	Prepare enough coals for a medium-hot fire or set a gas grill to medium-high.

4.	Remove the chicken thighs from the marinade and discard this marinade.

5.	Grill the thighs over medium-high heat for 35 to 40 minutes. During the last 10 minutes of cooking, turn them frequently to avoid excessive charring and mop often with the reserved marinade.

6.	Serve with the Grapefruit Mojo on the side (recipe follows).

Grapefruit Mojo
MAKES ABOUT 1 CUP

¹/₃ cup extra-virgin olive oil // 8 cloves garlic, finely chopped // ¹/₃ cup freshly squeezed grapefruit juice (about 1 grapefruit) // ¹/₃ cup freshly squeezed lime juice (about 3 limes) // ¹/₄ cup chopped fresh mint // ¹/₄ cup chopped fresh coriander // 1 teaspoon chopped fresh or dried rosemary // ¹/₂ teaspoon ground cumin // ¹/₂ teaspoon salt

1. In a small saucepan, heat the olive oil over medium heat. Add the garlic and cook for 30 seconds more. Add the remaining ingredients, being careful as the oil might splatter.

2. Remove from heat and let the mixture cool to room temperature before serving, or transfer to a container, cover, and keep cold in a refrigerator or ice-filled cooler for up to 3 days.

Jerk Chicken

On a hot day on the Daytona infield, there is nothing like these magical island flavors to ease your spirit. To save time, prepare the Spicy Mango Ketchup at home and have it ready to serve with the chicken.

SERVES 4

FOR THE MARINADE

½ cup chopped onions // ½ cup chopped scallions, green parts only // ¼ cup Caribbean chili sauce made with Scotch Bonnet peppers // ¼ cup freshly squeezed lime juice (2 to 3 limes) // ¼ cup freshly squeezed orange juice (about 1 orange) // ¼ cup fresh parsley leaves // 2 tablespoons packed brown sugar // 2 tablespoons dried rosemary // 2 tablespoons dried basil // 2 tablespoons dried thyme // 2 tablespoons ground allspice // 2 tablespoons yellow mustard // 1 teaspoon salt

12 chicken thighs, skins removed

1.　In a large bowl, combine all the ingredients for the marinade.

2.　Put the chicken thighs in a resealable freezer bag. Pour in the marinade, making sure the thighs are coated on all sides. Keep cold in a refrigerator or ice-filled cooler for at least 1 hour and up to 4 hours, but no longer.

3.　Prepare enough coals for a medium fire or set a gas grill to medium.

4.　Remove the chicken thighs from the marinade and discard the marinade. Grill the chicken over medium-low heat, turning several times to cook evenly. Cook until the meat starts pulling away from the bone, about 1 hour.

5.　Serve with Spicy Mango Ketchup (recipe follows).

Spicy Mango Ketchup

MAKES ABOUT 1½ CUPS

1 mango, peeled, pitted, and cut into 1-inch pieces // ½ cup coarsely chopped onions // ¼ cup scallions, chopped // ¼ cup freshly squeezed orange juice (about 1 orange) // 2 tablespoons freshly squeezed lime juice (1 lime) // 2 cloves garlic, finely chopped // 1 tablespoon Caribbean chili sauce made with Scotch Bonnet peppers // ½ teaspoon salt

1. Measure all the ingredients into a blender or food processor fitted with the metal blade and pulse until just blended.

2. Serve immediately or cover and keep cold in a refrigerator or ice-filled cooler for up to 2 days.

Texas-style Barbecued Chicken

The Roush-Yates partnership is known for its ability to build some of the best engines in racing. The sauce recommended for this recipe requires the same kind of attention to detail, but it's definitely worth the effort.

If you need to put more half-chickens on the grill, just overlap them slightly.

SERVES 4

2 cups wood chips, preferably hickory or oak, or 6 to 8 hickory or other hardwood chunks, for grilling // 2 whole chickens, 4 to 5 pounds each (neck, giblets, and wings removed) // 2 cups Mario's Kick-ass Barbecue Sauce (recipe follows) or the same amount of **2 BROTHERS** Barbecue Sauce

FOR THE RUB

2 tablespoons paprika // 2 tablespoons garlic salt // 2 tablespoons packed brown sugar // 2 tablespoons dried oregano // 1 teaspoon ground cinnamon // 1 teaspoon ground cumin

1.　One to 4 hours before grilling, soak the wood chips in enough water to cover.

2.　In a small bowl, combine the ingredients for the rub.

3.　Place the chickens on a clean work surface. Cut each chicken in half and remove the back from both sides (see Note). Rub the halves all over with the spice rub, put the chicken on a platter, cover, and place in a refrigerator or ice-filled cooler until ready to cook or up to 4 hours.

4.　Prepare enough coals for a hot fire. While the coals are heating, drain the wood chips. Use 12-inch square sheets of aluminum foil to make 3 packages of chips. Poke some holes in the top of each package to release the smoke during cooking.

5.　Arrange the hot coals on one side of the coal grate in as compact a pile as possible. Place a packet of chips directly on the coals. Place a 9-by-12-inch aluminum pan on the opposite side of the coal grate and add 1 inch of water to the pan.

6.　Arrange the chicken on the grill rack opposite the coals. Cover the grill with the vent positioned over the chicken. Smoke for 40 minutes, adding more wood chips after the first 20 minutes of cooking.

7.　If using a smoker, follow the manufacturer's instructions.

8.　Remove the chickens and place each half on a large sheet of aluminum foil. Spread on a thick layer of the barbecue sauce and fold the foil to fully encase the chicken.

9. Return the foil-wrapped chicken to the cool side of the grill. Add a few more coals to the fire. Cover the grill and cook for 20 minutes more and then remove from heat.

10. The chicken will be juicy and moist when the foil is removed. Serve with more barbecue sauce.

NOTE: To split a chicken, lay it on a cutting board breast-side up with the legs pointing toward you. Using a large knife, cut along each side of the backbone, cutting from the front to the rear. Remove the backbone, the flip the chicken over so it is skin-side down. Now you can split the chicken in half by cutting through the breast cartilage. After splitting the chickens, be sure to thoroughly clean the work surface with soap and hot water.

Mario's Kick-ass Barbecue Sauce

MAKES 3 CUPS

1 medium onion, finely chopped // 6 cloves garlic, finely chopped // 2 cups ketchup // 3/4 cup freshly squeezed orange juice (about 2 oranges) // 1/4 cup water // 1/4 cup freshly squeezed lemon juice (about 2 lemons) // 2 tablespoons red wine vinegar // 2 tablespoons tomato paste // 2 tablespoons honey // 2 tablespoons packed brown sugar // 2 tablespoons molasses // 2 tablespoons Worcestershire sauce // 2 tablespoons Dijon-style mustard // 1 tablespoon chili powder // 1 teaspoon liquid smoke // 1 teaspoon ground cumin // 1 teaspoon Tabasco or other hot sauce // Pinch cinnamon // Pinch ground cloves

1. In a heavy-bottomed sauce pan, mix all the ingredients together and bring to a boil over medium heat. Reduce the heat to low and simmer for 10 minutes, stirring frequently.

2. Let cool and serve or keep cold in a refrigerator or ice-filled cooler for up to 1 week.

Brickyard Barbecued Game Hens

These birds are cooked under-the-brick-style, or *al mattone* as they say in Tuscany. You'll use a hot brick to cook both sides of the bird at the same time and seal in the juices. The herb/pesto rub makes them even tastier, so try to let the birds marinate overnight before cooking. As for "hot bricks," the August race at the Brickyard at Indy is exceptionally hot, perhaps the hottest of the year—hence, hot bricks.

SERVES 4

FOR THE RUB

2 tablespoons dried basil // 2 tablespoons dried rosemary // 2 tablespoons coarsely chopped garlic // 2 tablespoons black pepper // 2 teaspoons salt // 1/4 cup extra-virgin olive oil

4 Rock Cornish game hens or poussins (baby chickens), backbones removed and birds flattened; or 4 half chickens // 1/2 cup extra-virgin olive oil // 4 house bricks wrapped in foil // 2 lemons for garnish

1. The night before cooking, in a medium bowl, mix the ingredients for the rub together. Place the birds skin-side down on a clean work surface and rub the inside of each with 2 tablespoons of the rub mix. Turn the birds skin-side up and do the same on the skin side.

2. Place the rubbed birds in a large bowl or container, seal, and keep cold in a refrigerator or ice-filled cooler overnight or up to 2 days.

3. When you are ready to cook the birds, prepare enough coals for a medium-hot fire. Arrange the coals so one side of the grill gets hot and the other side medium. If using a gas grill, set one side to hot, the other to medium.

4. Heat the foil-wrapped bricks on the hot side of the grill for 10 minutes.

5. While the bricks are heating, remove the birds from the container and brush them all over with olive oil.

6. Place birds skin-side down on the hot side of the grill and place a heated brick on top of each bird. Do not move the birds for a full 8 minutes, unless a flame-up occurs. (If this happens, cover the grill briefly to smother.)

7. Turn the birds skin-side up and cook for 10 minutes more under the heated brick over the hot side of the grill, then move them to the medium side and cook 10 minutes more.

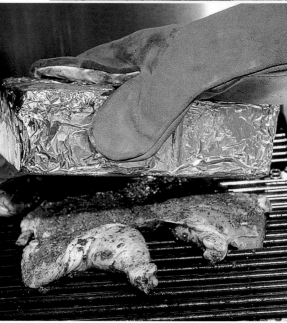

8. Turn the birds skin-side down, place back on the hot side under brick and cook 5 minutes. Turn them skin-side up and cook 5 minutes more.

9. The birds are done when a meat thermometer inserted into the thickest part of the thigh registers 170°F. Remove the birds to a platter and let rest for 5 minutes.

10. Garnish with lemon wedges and serve.

5-Spice Chicken

Say, by some fluke, you get a couple of hot passes laid on you for the race. Instead of hanging around the camper all afternoon playing horseshoes, you're walking through the pits and the garage area, watching all the action, seeing up close not only the drivers, but the crew chiefs you've heard about for so many years.

But while you're exalting in this behind-the-scenes adventure, nothing is happening with dinner. Fear not. You can make this chicken hours in advance and then let it just sit and get sauced in its sauce, secure in the knowledge that the longer you wait trying to track down Kasey Kahne so he can autograph the back of Grandma's shirt, the better the chicken will taste.

SERVES 6

6 boneless, skinless chicken breasts, flattened to $1/2$-inch thickness // 1 tablespoon vegetable oil // Salt and freshly ground black pepper // $1/2$ cup freshly squeezed orange juice (about 2 oranges) // 2 tablespoons honey // 1 tablespoon chopped fresh ginger // 1 teaspoon Chinese 5-spice powder // $1/2$ teaspoon wasabi powder // 4 scallions, finely chopped

1. Prepare enough coals for a hot fire or set a gas grill to high.

2. Place the chicken breasts on a clean work surface, rub with oil, and season with salt and pepper.

3. Grill the breasts over high heat, turning once, until they are golden brown and cooked through, about 7 minutes.

4. Let the breasts cool for a few minutes, then cut into 1-inch strips. Transfer to a large serving bowl.

5. In a small bowl, combine the remaining ingredients. Pour the mixture over the chicken and toss to evenly coat.

6. Serve immediately or cover with plastic and keep cold in a refrigerator or ice-filled cooler for up to 6 hours. Serve cold or let the chicken come to room temperature before serving.

Jambalaya Turkey Burger

You'll discover a little taste of New Orleans in these quick and easy burgers. Be sure to coat each patty with spray oil before putting them on the grill to keep them from sticking.

MAKES 4 BURGERS

1 pound ground turkey // 2 spicy smoked chicken sausages (about 3 ounces each), cut into 1/4-inch pieces // 1/4 cup finely chopped onion // 4-ounce jar roasted red peppers, drained and finely chopped // 3 tablespoons finely chopped garlic // 2 tablespoons chili powder // 1/2 teaspoon finely chopped jalapeño pepper (optional) // 1/2 teaspoon dried thyme // Freshly ground black pepper // Unflavored spray oil for grilling

8 slices white bread or 4 hamburger buns // Lettuce leaves // Red onion slices // Jarred salsa

1.	Place the ground turkey in a medium bowl. Add the remaining ingredients (except the spray oil) and gently mix together until just combined. Shape the mixture into four 3/4-inch-thick-by-4-inch patties (don't fret about how uniform they are). Put the patties on a flat platter, cover, and keep cold in a refrigerator or ice-filled cooler for 1 hour or up to 12 hours.

2.	Prepare enough coals for a medium-hot fire or set a gas grill to medium-high.

3.	Just before cooking, remove the patties from the refrigerator or cooler and liberally spray one side with the unflavored oil. Grill the burgers, sprayed sides down, over medium-high heat for 6 to 7 minutes.

4.	Spray the top sides of the burgers with the oil, being careful not to spray into the coals. Flip the burgers and grill until they are cooked through and no longer pink in the center, 6 to 7 minutes more .

5.	Put each burger in a bun and serve with lettuce, onion, and salsa.

Monster Shrimp

with Orange Chili Glaze

These are big shrimp, the ones that ate the other shrimp. When they opened the cage door after the death match, these are the shrimp that walked out of the ring.

Don't turn your back on the grill while you're cooking these—someone's liable to abscond with them.

SERVES 6

¹/₂ cup freshly squeezed orange juice (about 2 oranges) // ¹/₂ cup fresh cilantro // 1 tablespoon Asian red chili paste // ¹/₄ cup extra-virgin olive oil // 2 garlic cloves // 3 scallions, green parts only, cut into 1-inch pieces // 1 chipotle chile in adobo sauce // ¹/₂ teaspoon salt // 2 pounds extra-large shrimp (16 to 20-count size), shelled and deveined

1. Put the orange juice, cilantro, chili paste, olive oil, garlic, scallion, chipotle, and salt in a blender or food processor fitted with the metal blade and blend until smooth.

2. Place the shrimp in a resealable freezer bag and pour the orange juice mixture over the shrimp. Chill in a refrigerator or ice-filled cooler for 2 to 3 hours but no longer.

3. Remove the shrimp from the marinade and discard the marinade.

4. Grill the shrimp over medium-high heat until they are opaque in the centers, 3 to 4 minutes per side.

5. Remove from heat and serve immediately—though they still rock at room temperature.

Shrimp al ajillo

You can make this Spanish shrimp with garlic sauce when you need something dazzling in a hurry. If you buy the shrimp already cleaned, the dish goes together in about as much time as the average pit stop—all right, a pit stop where the crew also has to put in a round of wedge.

SERVES 6

¼ cup extra-virgin olive oil // ¼ cup (½ stick) butter // 2 pounds shrimp (16 to 20-count size), peeled and deveined // 6 cloves garlic, peeled and thinly sliced // ¼ cup freshly squeezed lemon juice (about 2 lemons) // 1 teaspoon paprika // ½ teaspoon red pepper flakes // 1 bunch parsley, roughly chopped // 1 teaspoon salt // Freshly ground black pepper

1.　Prepare enough coals for a medium-hot fire or set a gas grill to medium-high. Heat a skillet, preferably cast iron, on the grill. Add the olive oil and 1 tablespoon of the butter. When the butter melts, add the shrimp and garlic and sauté quickly until the shrimp are opaque in the middle, 5 to 6 minutes.

2.　Add the remaining butter, lemon juice, paprika, pepper flakes, ½ of the parsley, salt, and pepper to taste.

3.　When the butter has melted, stir everything together and transfer to a serving dish. Sprinkle on the remaining parsley and serve at once.

Spicy Beer Shrimp Boil

You'll like this dish because the guests do all the work peeling the shrimp and you just supply napkins.

SERVES 8

Three 12-ounce cans beer // 2 tablespoons cider vinegar // 1 tablespoon sweet paprika // 1 tablespoon garlic powder // 1 tablespoon cayenne // 1 tablespoon salt // 1 lemon, thinly sliced // 2 bay leaves // 2 teaspoons celery seeds // 3 pounds large shrimp (26 to 30-count size)

1.   Prepare enough coals for a hot fire or set a gas grill to high (or turn on the stove).
2.   In a large pot, combine all the ingredients except the shrimp and bring to a boil over high heat. Add the shrimp and stir once.
3.   Cover the pot and bring the liquid to a boil again. Then remove the cover and reduce the heat to medium-high. Simmer until the shrimp are cooked through, about 6 minutes.
4.   Use a slotted spoon to transfer the shrimp to a large serving platter. Serve immediately with either Classic or Bayou Cocktail Sauce. Or both (recipes follow).

Classic Cocktail Sauce
MAKES 1 CUP

3/4 cup ketchup // 1/4 cup prepared salsa // 2 tablespoons prepared horseradish // 2 tablespoons freshly squeezed lemon juice // 1 tablespoon Worcestershire sauce

1.   Mix all the ingredients together well and serve or cover and keep cold in a refrigerator or ice-filled cooler for up to 3 days.

Bayou Cocktail Sauce
MAKES 1 CUP

1/2 cup mayonnaise // 2 tablespoons ketchup // 1 tablespoon Worcestershire sauce // 1 tablespoon prepared white horseradish // 1/2 teaspoon celery seed // Dash Tabasco or other hot sauce

1.   Mix all the ingredients together well and serve or cover and keep cold in a refrigerator or ice-filled cooler for up to 3 days.

Salmon Hobo Packs

In Italy, we call these *salmone in cartoccio*. The preparation method makes for tender, intensely flavored fish. Since the fish are cooked wrapped in foil, you won't consternate a steak or burger that might happen to be sizzling on the other side of the grill.

SERVES 4

¼ cup soy sauce // 2 tablespoons vegetable oil // 2 tablespoons freshly squeezed lime juice (1 lime) //
2 tablespoons sesame oil // 2 tablespoons fresh ginger, finely chopped, or 1 teaspoon dried //
2 tablespoons olive oil // 2 medium onions, thinly sliced // 4 salmon fillets about 6 ounces each //
2 lemons, thinly sliced

1. In a small bowl, mix together the soy sauce, vegetable oil, lime juice, sesame oil, and ginger and set aside.

2. Cut four 16-inch pieces of foil and place them on a clean work surface. Brush the center of each piece of foil with some of the olive oil.

3. Prepare enough coals for a medium-hot fire or set a gas grill to medium-high.

4. Arrange ¼ of the onion slices on each piece of foil in roughly the shape of a fillet. Place the fillets over the onions.

5. Spoon ¼ of the soy sauce mixture evenly over the salmon. Put 4 or 5 lemon slices over the sauce.

6. Bring the long ends of one of the foil pieces together and fold tightly several times. Then fold up the sides to make a neat, sealed packet. Repeat to make four packets.

7. Place the packets on the grill and cook over medium-high heat until the fillets are opaque in the center and just cooked through, about 12 minutes.

8. Remove from heat and open the packets carefully, to avoid the escaping steam, and serve.

Soft-shelled Crab Sandwiches

with Spicy Tartar Sauce

Soft-shelled crabs are just good ol' blue crabs that have conveniently shed their shells while molting. They are in season only from May to early June, which overlaps several races. At the track, I like to eat them between some white bread with some spicy tartar sauce (much like SpongeBob prefers to eat his Krabbie Patties). They also make a great breakfast.

SERVES 4

FOR THE TARTAR SAUCE

3/4 cup mayonnaise // 3 tablespoons freshly squeezed lime juice (about 1 lime) // 2 tablespoons finely chopped parsley // 2 tablespoons finely chopped scallions // 1 tablespoon prepared relish // 1 teaspoon hot sauce // 1/2 teaspoon salt

1 cup milk // 2 eggs // 4 dashes hot sauce // 2 cups flour // 2 tablespoons Old Bay seasoning // 8 soft-shell crabs, cleaned (see Note) // 1/4 cup extra-virgin olive oil // 2 tablespoons butter // 16 slices white bread for serving

1. **TO MAKE THE TARTAR SAUCE:** In a medium bowl, mix all the ingredients together. Keep cold in a refrigerator or ice-filled cooler up to 2 days.

2. **TO MAKE THE CRABS:** In a medium bowl, combine the milk, eggs, and hot sauce. Measure the flour and Old Bay seasoning into another bowl and whisk to combine.

3. Prepare enough coals for a medium-hot fire or set a gas grill to medium-high.

4. While the coals are heating, dredge the crabs in the flour, shake off the excess, dunk them in the milk mixture, then dredge a second time in the flour. Place the floured crabs on a large platter.

5. Place a skillet, preferably cast iron, on the grill. Add one-half of the olive oil and 1 tablespoon of the butter. When the butter melts, sauté 4 of the crabs for 3 to 4 minutes per side until they are golden brown.

6. Transfer the cooked crabs to paper towels to drain and repeat with the remaining 4 crabs.

7. Serve the crabs warm between the bread with some of the tartar sauce.

NOTE: Most soft-shell crabs are sold already cleaned. If you're not sure, ask the fish monger and, if necessary, he'll clean them for you.

Grilled Lobsters
with Limoncello Vinaigrette

When it comes to their cars, race teams are required to follow NASCAR regulations. Wheel base: 110 inches. Height: 51 inches. Width: 72.5 inches. Weight: 3,400 pounds without the driver.

For tailgating menus there are no regulations. You can even serve lobsters—so why not?

SERVES 4

Limoncello Vinaigrette (recipe follows) // 4 live lobsters, 1½ pounds each (see note) // Extra virgin olive oil // Salt and freshly ground black pepper

1. Have ready the Limoncello Vinaigrette.

2. Prepare enough coals for a medium-hot fire or, when ready to grill, set a gas grill to medium-high.

3. To slay and split a lobster, hold it firmly with one hand at the intersection of its tail and body. Firmly insert a large knife (blade facing away from your hand) into the center of the shell just behind the head and cut through toward the top of the head. Turn the lobster 180 degrees and cut down through the tail. You should end up with two roughly equal halves. Repeat until all the lobsters are dead and in half.

4. Clean out the head sacs.

5. Place the lobster halves shell sides down on the grill over medium-high heat. Cook for 5 minutes.

6. Brush the tops with oil and sprinkle with salt and pepper. Turn shell sides up and cook for 5 minutes more until the meat is white and opaque.

7. Transfer to individual plates and serve immediately with Limoncello Vinaigrette.

NOTE: When buying your lobsters, look to get not just "live" lobsters, but lively ones. They should flip their tails and act a little agitated when lifted from the water. This means they are fresher and their meat will be tastier. Of course, bigger lobsters are meatier and you should feel free to indulge yourself, if you're feeling flush, by getting one 2-pounder per person. (Adjust the cooking time a few minutes longer to accommodate.) Lobsters will stay alive up to 48 hours out of the water, but they should be kept cold in a heavy paper grocery bag (not plastic). The quicker you cook them, though, the better, so think about picking up your lobsters on your way to the track.

Limoncello Vinaigrette

MAKES ABOUT ¾ CUP

¼ cup limoncello // 1 teaspoon grated lemon zest // 1 teaspoon salt // ½ teaspoon Dijon-style mustard // ½ cup extra-virgin olive oil

1.   In a medium bowl, whisk together the limoncello, lemon zest, salt, and mustard. Slowly drizzle in the olive oil as you continue whisking.

2.   Cover and keep cold in a refrigerator or ice-filled cooler until ready to use or for up to 2 days. Let the vinaigrette come to room temperature before serving.

5

Chili, Stew,
AND OTHER STUFF
COOKED IN A POT

Between shopping for racing paraphernalia, visiting the exhibits, checking out the NASCAR Channel live taping, and running into a steady stream of racing buddies, it's a busy weekend.

That's when having a pot of chili or stew already cooked and sitting in the fridge or ice cooler can come in very handy.

The flavor of a chili or stew actually improves with a day or two in the refrigerator. You're doing both yourself and the chili a favor by making it in advance. Be sure to stir it often when reheating so as not to scorch the bottom of the chili or stew.

Restrictor Plate Chili

Meaning this one is on the mild side, full of flavor but not too spicy. The kids will probably eat a lot of it, so make sure you prepare enough.

SERVES 8

6 slices bacon, cut into 1-inch pieces // 2 onions, finely chopped // 2 red bell peppers, stemmed, seeded, and finely chopped // 6 cloves garlic, finely chopped // 2 pounds ground sirloin // 6-ounce can tomato paste // ¼ cup chili powder // 2 tablespoons ground cumin // Two 4-ounce cans diced green chiles, drained // 4-ounce can diced jalapeño chiles // 4 cups water // 28-ounce can crushed tomatoes // 1 cup coarsely chopped pitted green olives // 1 teaspoon ground cinnamon // 2 tablespoons dried oregano // 12-ounce can pinto beans, drained // 12-ounce can corn, drained

1. Prepare enough coals for a medium-hot fire or set a gas grill to medium-high (or turn on the stove).

2. Place a large pot over medium-high heat and add the bacon pieces. When the bacon is cooked through, about 6 minutes, pour out some of the fat, add the onion and red bell peppers, and cook until the vegetables soften, about 6 minutes more. Add the garlic and cook for 1 minute more.

3. Add the ground sirloin and cook, breaking up the sirloin, until all the pink is gone, about 5 minutes more.

4. Add the tomato paste, chili powder, and ground cumin and cook for 1 minute, stirring often.

5. Add the green chiles, jalapeños, water, tomatoes, olives, cinnamon, and oregano and bring the liquid to a boil. Reduce the heat to medium-low, cover, and simmer the chili for 1 hour, stirring every 20 minutes or so to keep the bottom from scorching.

6. Add the pinto beans and corn and simmer for 10 minutes more, stirring often. Remove from heat and serve, or let cool and keep cold in a refrigerator or ice-filled cooler for up to 3 days.

7. Reheat the chili by placing the pot on the grill over medium heat, stirring to keep the bottom from scorching, until the chili is heated through.

Venison Chili

If you are a regular fan of Wally Dallenbach's hunting show, chances are you've got a freezer full of venison you don't know what to do with. Here's an easy way to start using it up.

SERVES 6

4 tablespoons vegetable oil // 1½ pounds ground venison // 1 onion, finely chopped // 4 cloves garlic, finely chopped // 1 tablespoon chili powder // 1 tablespoon dried oregano // 2 teaspoons ground cumin // ½ teaspoon ground cinnamon // ½ teaspoon ground allspice // 1 can (15 ounces) crushed tomatoes // 1 cup red wine // 1 teaspoon salt // 1 teaspoon freshly ground black pepper

1. Place a large pot over medium-high heat, add 2 tablespoons of the oil and the venison and cook until the meat is no longer pink, about 6 minutes. Transfer the venison to a large bowl, return the pot to the heat, add the remaining oil and the onion pieces and cook, stirring often, until the onions are soft, about 8 minutes. Add the garlic and cook for 1 minute more.

2. Add the chili powder, oregano, cumin, cinnamon, and allspice and cook for 1 minute more, stirring continuously.

3. Return the venison to the pot and add the tomatoes, wine, salt, and pepper. Raise the heat to high and bring the liquid to a boil. Immediately reduce the heat to low, cover, and simmer for 45 minutes, stirring occasionally to keep the bottom from scorching.

4. Let cool and keep cold in the refrigerator for up to 3 days.

5. Reheat at the tailgate on the grill over medium heat, stirring occasionally to prevent scorching.

Leo's Sloppy Joes

This is my son Leo's favorite dish, which he likes to make himself. He personally recommends it to all young NASCAR fans. The kids in your crew might want to give it a try (with an adult assistant chef, especially if the cooking will be done outside on a grill where the neighbor's kids can see them).

SERVES 4

2 tablespoons vegetable oil // 1½ pounds ground round // 5 tablespoons tomato paste // 2 tablespoons sugar // 12-ounce jar mild salsa // 4 sandwich rolls, sliced, or 8 slices white bread for serving

1. Place a skillet over medium-high heat and let it get hot for about a minute. Alternatively, prepare enough coals for a medium-hot fire or set a gas grill to medium-high. (When the coals are ready, arrange them so one side of the grill is medium-hot, the other side medium.) Add the oil to the pan and spread it to cover the bottom of the pan.

2. Add the ground round and cook, breaking up the meat with the back of a spoon, until all the pink is gone, about 15 minutes.

3. Add the remaining ingredients (except the rolls) one at a time and stir slowly to combine.

4. When the liquid starts to simmer, reduce the heat to low (or slide the pan to the cooler side of the grill), partially cover, and simmer for 45 minutes. Stir occasionally to keep the bottom from scorching.

5. Open a roll or arrange 2 slices of the white bread on a plate. Spoon the meat mixture over it and serve. Repeat to make 4 Joes.

Corona
Corona
Corona
DISCOUNT
TIRE CO.
DODGE
DISCOUNT
TIRE CO.
DODGE
GOODYEAR
36
36
123

Cocido Bogotano

This is a classic stew from Bogota, Columbia. Though it has a long list of ingredients, it's a snap to prepare at home. It has nothing to do with NASCAR, but if you show up with it at a tailgate—maybe the Telcel Motorola 200 in Mexico City—everyone will be very, very happy.

SERVES 8

2 tablespoons extra-virgin olive oil // 1 large onion, coarsely chopped // 1 cup canned plum tomatoes, drained // 2 pounds boneless beef for stew, preferably chuck, cut into 1½-inch cubes // 3 medium yams or sweet potatoes, peeled, and cut into ¾-inch cubes // 4 carrots, peeled, trimmed, and cut into ½-inch slices // 3 cloves garlic, coarsely chopped // 1 bay leaf // 1 teaspoon ground cumin // 1 teaspoon dried oregano // ½ teaspoon red chile flakes // 2 cups water // 1 cup white wine or dry vermouth // 1 tablespoon cider vinegar // 12-ounce package frozen peas // 4 ears corn, shucked, and cut into 2-inch lengths // Salt and freshly ground black pepper

1. Place a heavy, 3- to 4-quart Dutch oven over medium-high heat. Alternatively, prepare enough coals for a medium-hot fire or set a gas grill to medium-high. (When the coals are ready, arrange them so one side of the grill is medium-hot, the other side medium.)

2. Add the olive oil and the onions to the Dutch oven and cook, stirring, until the onions begin to soften, about 4 minutes.

3. Stir in the tomatoes and cook 3 minutes more. Add the meat, yams, carrots, garlic, bay leaf, cumin, oregano, red chile flakes, water, wine, and vinegar. Bring the liquid to a boil, then immediately reduce the heat to low (or slide the pot to the cooler side of the grill) and simmer, covered, for 45 minutes.

4. Add the peas and corn and cook 25 minutes more. Season with salt and pepper to taste and remove from heat.

5. Let the stew cool and keep cold in the refrigerator overnight to let the flavor develop.

6. At the tailgate, reheat on a grill over medium heat.

Pork Shoulder Braciolona

As much as I love a grilled steak when I'm tailgating at the track, I do sometimes yearn for something that has more of a classic Italian flavor. Pork braciolona satisfies that craving, and a few others as well. It affords an opportunity to transform your grill into the kitchen of a cozy hosteria in Umbria. It's also a great dish to make early in the day and serve at room temp later, allowing for relaxation come dinnertime.

SERVES 8

3 pound piece of pork shoulder or leg, butterflied open, and pounded to yield one large piece, about 1½ inches thick and 12 inches square (ask your butcher to do this for you) // Kosher salt and freshly ground black pepper // 1 bunch Italian parsley, finely chopped // ½ cup pine nuts // ½ cup dried currants // ½ cup freshly grated Parmigiano-Reggiano or Parmesan cheese // 16 slices prosciutto (about ⅓ pound) // 4 hardboiled eggs, peeled and quartered lengthwise // Several gratings of nutmeg // 4 tablespoons dried oregano // ¼ cup extra-virgin olive oil // 2 red onions, finely chopped // 4 garlic cloves, thinly sliced // 2 cups dry white wine // Three 28-ounce cans crushed Italian tomatoes with juice // 2 teaspoons red chile flakes // Butcher twine for tying meat

1. Place the pork on a cutting board and season it with salt and pepper.

2. In a medium bowl, stir together the parsley, pine nuts, currants and Parmigiano-Reggiano and season with salt and pepper.

3. Lay the prosciutto slices over the pork to cover completely. Sprinkle the parsley mixture evenly over the prosciutto. Arrange the eggs in two rows across the meat. Grate nutmeg over everything and sprinkle with 2 tablespoons of the oregano, rubbing it between your fingers to release the essential oils.

4. Carefully roll the pork up like a jellyroll and tie firmly with butcher twine in several places. Season the roll with salt and pepper. (If making ahead, you can keep cold in a refrigerator or an ice-filled cooler for up to 2 days.)

5. Place an 8-quart Dutch oven on high heat, add the olive oil and heat until smoking. Carefully brown the pork roll on all sides, taking your time to get a deep golden brown, 15 to 20 minutes. Remove the meat and set aside.

6. Lower the heat slightly, add the onions, remaining 2 tablespoons of oregano, and the garlic to the pan and cook until lightly browned and soft, about 8 minutes.

7. Add the wine, tomatoes, and red chile flakes and bring to a boil. Return the pork to the pan and simmer, with the pan partially covered for 1 hour and 20 minutes, moving occasionally to prevent sticking.

8. Let the pork cook in the juices, then place in a refrigerator or ice-filled cooler for at least 4 hours and up to 24 hours. Let the meat come to room temperature before either reheating on the grill or slicing and serving. Make sure everyone gets some sauce spooned over their meat.

6

Vegetables and Sides

During race weekend, green vegetables tend to take a back seat to every other known food group. And, as race cars have no back seat, they tend not to appear, even in spirit.

(Beer, though it is made with hops, is not a vegetable.) But you'll definitely want to think about having some potatoes, corn, a pan of Spanish rice, or a skillet of Spiked Beans as part of your meals.

Potato Packets

Fit these in the empty spaces on the grill where you're not cooking something else and you'll have perfect potatoes. They take 40 minutes to cook, so time the rest of the meal accordingly.

SERVES 4

8 slices uncooked bacon // 2 medium onions, thinly sliced // 4 large potatoes, scrubbed and thinly sliced // 4 tablespoons (½ stick) butter // Salt // Freshly ground black pepper // 2 tablespoons extra virgin olive oil

1. On a clean work surface, lay out a double layer of aluminum foil, about 14 inches long.

2. Place 2 slices of bacon in the center, then 2 slices of onion, then about ½ a potato's worth of potato slices. Top with a tablespoon of butter and season with salt and pepper. Repeat the layering of ingredients to make a second pile on top of the first. Drizzle 1 tablespoon of olive oil over everything.

3. Fold the long ends of the foil over the top, double the fold to make a seal, and then neatly fold up the sides.

4. Assemble a second packet with the remaining ingredients.

5. Place each potato packet on the grill over medium-high heat, until the potatoes are cooked through, about 40 minutes. (You'll have to open one of the packets to check—it's the only way I've figured out how to see if they're done. Be careful of the escaping steam.)

6. Remove the potatoes from the foil and serve.

Italian Potato Salad

While I do like a helping of classic mayo-based potato salad, I'm also a big fan of this one, which has olive oil for dressing and gets a little boost of power coming into the straightaway from the bacon.

SERVES 6

3 pounds small red potatoes, cut in half // 1 medium red onion, finely chopped // 3 celery stalks, finely chopped // 8 slices cooked bacon, crumbled into small pieces // 4-ounce jar roasted red peppers, drained and coarsely chopped // ¼ cup chopped parsley // ¼ cup chopped fresh basil, or 2 teaspoons dried // 2 teaspoons caraway seeds // ¼ cup extra-virgin olive oil // 2 tablespoons red wine vinegar // 1 teaspoon Dijon mustard // 1 teaspoon salt // ½ teaspoon freshly ground black pepper

I.   It's best to start this recipe at home. In a large saucepan, cover potatoes with cold water by an inch. Bring to a boil over medium-high heat. Reduce the heat to low and simmer until the potatoes are just cooked through, about 16 minutes. (They'll continue cooking a bit after you remove them from the pot.) Drain well in a colander and let cool, gently turning the potatoes with a rubber spatula to allow the bottom ones to cool as well.

2.   Add the onion, celery, bacon, red peppers, parsley, basil, caraway seeds, and salt and pepper to taste.

3.   In a small bowl, whisk together the olive oil, vinegar, mustard, and the salt and pepper. Pour the dressing over the potato mixture and gently toss.

4.   Serve immediately or keep cold in a refrigerator or ice-filled cooler, covered, for up to 1 day.

NOTE: You can prepare the potato mixture and dressing separately up to 2 days in advance. Keep cold in a refrigerator or ice-filled cooler, covering the potatoes with a clean, damp dishtowel.

cingular.com
rcrracing.com
jeffburton.com

Borlotti Beans with Balsamic Vinegar

You'll get rave reviews if you make this simple, rustic appetizer traditionally served in the Emilia-Romagna region of Italy. The unique flavor of the balsamic gives the beans a distinctive kick. If you shell out some big bucks for a 25- or 50-year-old balsamic, you'll experience one of the great flavors in the world.

SERVES 8

Two 12-ounce cans kidney (borlotti) beans // ¼ cup extra-virgin olive oil // 2 tablespoons balsamic vinegar // 3 cloves garlic, finely chopped // 1 tablespoon chopped fresh rosemary // ½ teaspoon freshly ground black pepper // Salt

1. Put all the beans in a colander, drain, and rinse gently. Transfer to a large bowl and add the olive oil, vinegar, garlic, rosemary, and black pepper. Season with salt to taste.

2. Let rest in the refrigerator for at least 1 hour and up to 12 hours before serving.

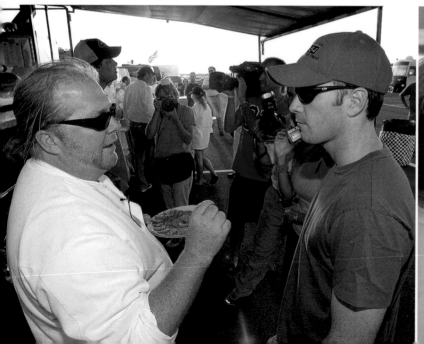

Spiked Beans

These are the kind of beans cowboys served out on the range around the campfire under the stars. The beans would then serenade the cowboys during the night, helping to keep the coyotes at bay.

SERVES 6

1 tablespoon extra-virgin olive oil // 1 medium onion, finely chopped // 4 cloves garlic, finely chopped // 1/4 pound Andouille or other spicy smoked sausage, cut into 1/2-inch pieces // 1/2 cup packed brown sugar // 1/2 cup ketchup // 2 tablespoons mustard // 2 tablespoons chili powder // 1 teaspoon ground cumin // 1/4 cup whiskey // 14-ounce can kidney beans, drained // 14-ounce can pinto beans, drained // 14-ounce can black-eyed peas, drained

1.   Prepare enough coals for a medium-hot fire and arrange them on one side of the grill or set a gas grill to medium-high.

2.   Place a large skillet, preferably cast iron, on the grill over the coals. Add the olive oil and onion and cook, stirring often, until the onion softens, about 5 minutes. Add the garlic and cook 1 minute more.

3.   Add the remaining ingredients and bring the mixture to a boil.

4.   Move the skillet to the side of the grill opposite the coals (or decrease the gas grill to medium-low), cover the skillet and grill, and cook for 20 minutes.

5.   Remove from heat and serve hot.

Roasted Corn with Chipotle Butter

Just like Jeff Gordon or Tony Stewart always finds a way to pass when there doesn't seem to be any room, so an experienced griller can find a little empty space on the grill for some corn. Don't be afraid to snap the ears in half if you have to fit them in between the steaks and the brats. Of course grilled corn is great the way it is, but the chipotle butter gives it an extra kick.

SERVES 6

1/2 cup butter (1 stick) at room temperature // 2 chipotle chiles, finely chopped // 1 teaspoon minced garlic // 1/2 teaspoon salt // 1/2 teaspoon freshly ground black pepper // 6 ears corn, husked

1. Put the butter, chipotles, garlic, salt, and pepper in a medium bowl. Use a fork to mash together until just combined. Transfer the mixture to a 12-inch strip of plastic wrap and use the wrap to roll the butter mixture into a log roughly the size of the original stick. Place the butter in a refrigerator or ice-filled cooler until ready to use.

2. Grill the corn over medium-high heat for 10 to 12 minutes, turning frequently as the bottoms turn golden brown.

3. Remove from heat and serve immediately with the Chipotle Butter on the side.

Corn and Sweet Onion Salad

This side salad is a great way to use up any leftover grilled corn. After you make it once, however, you'll be sure to throw a few extra ears on the fire to ensure you'll have leftovers.

SERVES 6

1/4 cup plus 2 tablespoons extra-virgin olive oil // 2 medium sweet onions, thinly sliced // 6 ears of corn, grilled, or 2 cans (8 ounces each) corn kernels packed in water, drained // 6-ounce jar roasted red peppers, drained and finely chopped // 12-ounce can white beans // 1/2 cup finely chopped fresh parsley // 2 tablespoons freshly squeezed lemon juice (1 lemon) // 2 tablespoons red wine vinegar // 2 tablespoons chopped fresh basil or 1 teaspoon dried // 1 tablespoon fresh thyme leaves or 1 teaspoon dried // 1 teaspoon sugar // 1 teaspoon salt // Freshly ground black pepper

1. Place a skillet over medium heat. Add 2 tablespoons of the olive oil and the onions and cook slowly until the onions start to caramelize, about 15 minutes. Remove from heat and transfer to a large mixing bowl.

2. Using a serrated knife, trim the kernels from the roasted corn and add to the bowl along with the roasted pepper, white beans, and parsley. Set aside.

3. In a small bowl, whisk together the lemon juice, vinegar, basil, thyme, sugar, salt, and pepper to taste. While you are whisking, slowly drizzle in the remaining 1/4 cup olive oil so it is well incorporated.

4. Pour the dressing over the vegetables and serve or cover and keep cold in a refrigerator or ice-filled cooler for up to 12 hours.

Sweet and Spicy Corn Muffins

These muffins are great to serve with anything that comes with barbecue sauce. It's best to prepare these at home and place in a sealed plastic container for transporting. The muffins will keep up to 24 hours.

MAKES 12 MUFFINS

Cooking grease for greasing pan // 1 cup unbleached all-purpose flour // 1 cup yellow cornmeal // 6 tablespoons sugar // 1 tablespoon baking powder // 1 teaspoon baking soda // 1½ teaspoons salt // 3 eggs // 1 cup sour cream // ½ cup (1 stick) butter, melted // 1 cup canned corn kernels packed in water, drained // 4-ounce can diced green chiles, drained // 1 jalapeño chile, stemmed, seeded, and finely chopped

1. Preheat the oven to 350°F. Lightly grease a 12-hole standard muffin pan.

2. In a large bowl, whisk together the flour, cornmeal, sugar, baking powder, baking soda, and salt until combined.

3. In a medium bowl, whisk together the eggs, sour cream, and melted butter. Stir in the corn, green chiles, and jalapeño.

4. Pour the wet ingredients into the dry and stir until just combined. Do not over mix.

5. Fill each muffin tin three quarters full of batter and bake on the center rack of the oven until a toothpick inserted into the center of the center muffin comes out clean, 18 to 20 minutes.

6. Remove from the oven and let the muffins cool in the pan on a rack. Run a small, clean knife around the edge of each muffin, invert the tin, and tip out the muffins.

7. To reheat the muffins on the grill, wrap them 4-to-6 at a time in aluminum foil and put them on the grill rack over medium heat for about 7 minutes. Remove from heat and serve immediately.

Refried Beans

Adrian Fernandez is Mexico's most revered race car driver. Fans and media surround him in his native country much like the paparazzi clamor over Brad and Angelina here in the states. Perhaps after mastering this refried beans recipe and serving it at a tailgate party in Mexico City, you can give Adrian a break and grab some media attention yourself.

SERVES 6

1/4 cup vegetable oil // 1 medium onion, finely chopped // 2 cloves garlic, finely chopped // 2 teaspoons ground cumin // 1 teaspoon chili powder // 1/2 teaspoon cinnamon // 1/2 teaspoon cayenne // 1/2 teaspoon salt // 4-ounce can chopped green chiles // Two 12-ounce cans pinto or kidney beans // Salt and freshly ground black pepper

1. Place a skillet, preferably cast iron, over medium-high heat and let it get hot. Add the oil and the onions and cook, stirring often, until the onions soften, about 8 minutes. Add the garlic, cumin, chili powder, cinnamon, cayenne, and salt and cook 1 minute more.

2. Add the green chiles and beans and cook until the beans are heated through, about 5 minutes.

3. Off the heat, use a potato masher to mash the mixture together until it is, well, mashed. Cease, however, before it becomes pureed.

4. Return the pan to the heat and cook until the beans are heated through, about 5 more minutes.

5. Remove from heat, season with salt and pepper, and serve.

Fire-roasted Onions

These go with just about anything you cook on the grill. They're so easy to make and take up so little room, there's no reason not to have them with pretty much any meal.

SERVES 8

4 large red onions // 8 tablespoons extra-virgin olive oil // 1 tablespoon chopped fresh or dried rosemary // 1 tablespoon chopped fresh thyme leaves or 1 teaspoon dried // Salt and freshly ground black pepper // Heavy-duty aluminum foil for grilling

1.　Halve the onions across the equator and place on a medium platter, cut-side up. Drizzle each onion half with 1 tablespoon olive oil and a pinch each of rosemary, thyme, salt, and pepper.

2.　Wrap the onions and herbs in a double-layer of heavy-duty aluminum foil. Place the wrapped onions flat side down onto the coals or on the top of the grill over medium-high heat and roast until the onions become tender, 20–30 minutes.

Creamy Coleslaw

A good coleslaw can serve as an all-purpose side dish. It goes with barbecue, with sandwiches, with grilled chicken, even with steaks.

SERVES 8

1 pound (about 1/2 medium head) cabbage // 1 medium onion, peeled and grated // 1 carrot, peeled and grated // 6 radishes, grated // 1/2 cup mayonnaise // 2 tablespoons red wine vinegar // 1 teaspoon celery seeds // 1 teaspoon salt // Freshly ground black pepper

1.　Quarter the cabbage head, trim off the core and remove the outer, dark green leaves. Cut each quarter across into the thinnest strips you can.

2.　Transfer the cabbage to a large mixing bowl. Add the onion, carrot, and radishes and toss together.

3.　Add the mayonnaise, vinegar, celery seeds, salt, and pepper to taste and gently toss with your hands, making sure the dressing is evenly distributed.

4.　Serve immediately or keep cold in a refrigerator or ice-filled cooler until ready to use, up to 48 hours.

7
Desserts

If you have kids in your tailgating crew, then you definitely need some desserts. If you don't have kids, then you'll need another reason. Like, for instance, it's your third race this year, or it's a month with an "R" in it, or you haven't had dessert since yesterday.

Dessert is the traditional burn out after the winner takes the checkered flag—the race isn't really over until you see it.

Most of these desserts are prepared ahead of time, so they are ready exactly when you are. The ones that require a little last minute prep are well worth the extra effort.

Strawberry Shortcakes

Sometimes I make my own shortcakes and sometimes I use store-bought ones, which I distress a little to make them look homemade.

SERVES 6

2 quarts ripe strawberries // 4 tablespoons sugar // 2 cups heavy cream // 1/2 teaspoon vanilla extract // 12 store-bought or handmade shortcakes (recipe follows)

1. Hull and wash the strawberries and slice them, but not too thinly.
2. Place 2 cups of the strawberry slices along with 2 tablespoons of the sugar in a large saucepan and cook over medium heat until the strawberries soften, about 8 minutes. Reduce the heat and simmer until the liquid thickens slightly, about 5 minutes. Let the mixture cool.
3. In a small, deep bowl, whip the cream until it holds soft peaks, then whip 1 minute more, adding the remaining 2 tablespoons of sugar.
4. Split the shortcakes. Top the bottom half with fresh strawberries and whipped cream. Place the top over this, top with more strawberries and whipped cream. Drizzle some of the cooked strawberry syrup over everything and get out of the way.

FOR THE SHORTCAKES

2 cups unbleached all-purpose flour // 4 tablespoons sugar // 4 teaspoons baking powder // 1/2 teaspoon salt // 5 tablespoons cold butter // 2 large eggs // 3/4 cup heavy cream

1. Preheat the oven to 450°F.
2. In a medium bowl, whisk together the flour, sugar baking powder, and salt.
3. Cut the butter into small pieces and add it to the flour mixture. Using your fingertips, rub the bits of butter together with some flour until they divide and are the size of split peas.
    In a medium bow, mix together the eggs and cream. Stir the wet mixture into the dry until it just comes together. Knead briefly. It should be just the tiniest bit sticky.
4. Transfer the dough to a cutting board or a clean work surface. Press the dough into a roughly 3/4-inch thick rectangle and cut into 2-inch rounds using a biscuit cutter or the top of a glass. Transfer the rounds to an ungreased baking sheet.
5. Gently shape the remaining dough into another rectangle and cut some more rounds. Repeat to use all of the dough.
6. Bake on the center rack of the oven until the shortcakes turn golden brown, 7 to 9 minutes.
7. Let them cool for 20 minutes before slicing in half.

Bananas Foster

This is a classic I learned from the master himself, Emeril Lagasse, who loves to wow my kids when we are visiting, doing a "flame on" routine just like the Human Torch.

The most important part of the flaming technique is to maintain a hot pan so the rum ignites. Make sure you have all the ingredients prepped and accessible, as once you start this recipe, you'll have to act fast. After serving these for dessert at dinner, you might get requests to make them again for breakfast the next day.

SERVES 4

4 bananas, ripe but not over-ripe // ¼ cup (½ stick) butter // 6 tablespoons packed brown sugar //
2 ounces rum, 151-proof // ½ teaspoon cinnamon // 4 scoops cold vanilla ice cream

1.   Heat a 12-inch skillet, preferably cast iron, over high heat until smoking.

2.   Meanwhile, peel and halve the bananas lengthwise. Put the butter in the pan. It should melt and start to brown quickly.

3.   Immediately add the brown sugar and stir to form a caramel-like sauce that bubbles quickly.

4.   Carefully pour in the rum and ignite with a match or tip the pan slightly to catch the flames from the grill.

5.   Immediately add the bananas and the cinnamon. When the flame subsides (after about 30 seconds), toss the bananas carefully to coat with the sauce and cook 2 minutes more.

6.   Put the ice cream in individual bowls, spoon on the bananas and sauce, and serve immediately.

Double Chocolate Time-trial Brownies

When speed is of the essence, these are the brownies for you. They're quick and easy to make and will disappear faster than donuts in the press box.

MAKES 9 GOOD-SIZE BROWNIES

Cooking grease for greasing pan // 1/2 cup (1 stick) butter, cut into 4 equal pieces // 1/2 cup Dutch-process unsweetened cocoa powder // 1 cup granulated sugar // 8 ounces chocolate chips // 1 teaspoon real vanilla extract // 2 extra-large eggs // 3/4 cup unbleached all-purpose flour // Confectioners' sugar for topping

I.   Preheat the oven to 325°F. Grease an 8-by-8-inch baking pan.

2.   In a small saucepan over medium-low heat, melt the butter and cocoa powder, stirring continuously until the butter is just melted. Use a rubber spatula to transfer the cocoa mixture to a large mixing bowl.

3.   Let the cocoa mixture cool for 2 minutes. Then add the sugar, chocolate chips, and vanilla and stir with a wooden spoon until combined. Add the eggs 1 at a time, stirring so that each is well combined. Add the flour and stir until just combined. Do not over-mix.

4.   Transfer the batter to the prepared pan and bake on the center rack for 22 minutes or until a toothpick inserted in the center comes out clean or with tiny crumbs.

5.   Dust with confectioners' sugar, cut into 9 squares, and serve. Or, store for up to 2 days in a tightly-sealed plastic container.

Mudslide Pie

At the moment, it's common for a winning driver to pop open bottles of champagne to celebrate a victory with his crew. But that's only because they haven't yet tasted Mudslide Pie.

SERVES 6

20 graham crackers, finely crushed to yield about 1¼ cups crumbs // ¼ cup (½ stick) butter, melted // 1 quart coffee or chocolate ice cream, softened // 1 cup whipped cream // ½ cup fudge ice cream topping // 4 Oreo Cookies, coarsely crushed // 6 ounces white chocolate, coarsely chopped

1. In a medium bowl, mix the graham cracker crumbs and the butter until well blended. Transfer to a 9-inch pie plate and use your fingertips to press the mixture firmly onto the bottom and sides of the pan to form a crust.

2. Spread the ice cream into the crust. Freeze at least 6 hours or until firm.

3. Remove the pie from the freezer and top with the whipped cream just before serving. Then drizzle on the fudge topping, sprinkle with the crushed cookies and white chocolate pieces, and stand back to watch the fun begin.

Rocky Road Bread Pudding

Being in the marbles is, as you know, not where you want your car to be running. This rocky road offers as smooth and delicious a ride as you can find.

SERVES 8

Cooking grease for greasing pan // 3 cups whole milk // 6 ounces bittersweet chocolate //
1/4 cup (1/2 stick) butter // 1/2 cup sugar // pinch salt // 8 slices white bread, cut into roughly
1-inch pieces // 3 large eggs // 6 ounces chocolate chips // 4 ounces walnuts, coarsely chopped //
1 cup mini marshmallows // 1/2 cup raisins // 1/4 cup bourbon (optional)

1.   Preheat the oven to 350°F. Grease a 10-inch skillet, preferably cast iron.

2.   In a small saucepan over low heat combine the milk, chocolate, butter, sugar, and salt. Heat, stirring continuously, until the butter and chocolate are just melted.

3.   Put the pieces of bread in the skillet and pour on the milk mixture, making sure all the bread is covered. Let rest for 5 minutes.

4.   In a small bowl, beat the eggs and then stir them into the bread mixture to combine well.

5.   Put the skillet in a large roasting pan and place on the center rack of the oven, then pour hot water into the roasting pan to within 1 inch of the top of the skillet.

6.   Carefully slide in the rack and bake for 40 minutes.

7.   Meanwhile, in a large bowl, mix together the chocolate chips, walnuts, marshmallows, and raisins. Add the bourbon, if desired, and toss together.

8.   After the pudding has baked 40 minutes, spread the chocolate chip mixture evenly over the top. Continue baking until a toothpick inserted in the center of the pudding comes out clean or with a few specks attached, 10 to 15 minutes more. The pudding should still be a bit wobbly.

9.   Serve warm, if possible, or cover the skillet in foil and store in the refrigerator or an ice-filled chest for up to 24 hours.

NOTE: To reheat, place the foil-covered skillet on the grill after you have finished cooking and let the dying coals gently heat up the pudding. Or, reheat on a gas grill set to low.

Key Lime Pie

I find Key Lime pie goes with just about any grilled food. On a hot day, it's good just by itself. I like leftover Key Lime pie for breakfast. Sometimes I have pie for breakfast and serve the leftovers, if there are any, for dessert. Sometimes I just double the recipe to make two pies, which seems as easy as making one.

SERVES 6

4 large egg yolks // 15-ounce can sweetened condensed milk // ½ cup freshly squeezed lime juice (about 4 limes) // 1 prepared graham cracker crust

1. Preheat the oven to 350°F.

2. Put the egg yolks into a medium mixing bowl. Beat briefly on medium speed with a hand-held mixer. With the mixer on, slowly pour in the condensed milk, then continue beating until the mixture lightens, about 2 minutes. Continue mixing and dribble in the lime juice until entirely incorporated.

3. Use a rubber spatula to transfer the mixture into the prepared crust and bake on the center rack of the oven for 18 minutes or until the pie is completely set.

4. Let cool for several hours before cutting and serving.

5. Cover the pie with aluminum foil and store in the refrigerator or an ice-filled cooler for up to 48 hours. Be careful not to put anything on top of the pie or it will leave a distinct impression in the filling.

Chocolate Pecan Pie

Nut lovers will go nuts for this pie. If someone in your crew doesn't fancy nuts, well, they're nuts.

SERVES 6

FOR THE CRUST

1 cup flour // 1/4 cup sugar // 1/2 cup (1 stick) butter, cut into 1/2-inch slices // 1 egg yolk //
4 tablespoons ice water

1.   Put all the ingredients for the crust in the bowl of a food processor fitted with the metal blade and pulse until the ingredients come together in a ball.

2.   Refrigerate for 1 hour but no longer than 24 hours before rolling out for crust.

3.   Roll out the crust between two layers of wax paper until it is slightly larger than the circumference of the pie plate.

4.   Remove the top layer of wax paper and gently flip the crust onto the pie plate. Now remove the remaining layering of wax paper. Pinch the edges of the crust so it fits neatly in the pie plate and looks nice.

FOR THE PECAN PIE

10 tablespoons (1 stick plus 2 tablespoons) butter, softened // 3/4 cup packed brown sugar //
3 large eggs // 1 cup dark corn syrup // 1 cup whole pecan halves // 6 ounces bittersweet chocolate, chopped into chip-size pieces // 1 teaspoon vanilla extract

1.   Preheat the oven to 450°F.

2.   Put the butter in a large mixing bowl and add the sugar. Stir continuously with a wooden spoon until the mixture is smooth, about 3 minutes. Add the eggs one at a time, beating at each addition until incorporated. Add the remaining ingredients.

3.   Pour the filling into the pastry-lined pie pan. Bake on the center rack of the oven for 10 minutes, then reduce the heat to 350°F and bake until the pie is set and a toothpick inserted in the center comes out clean, 30-35 minutes more.

4.   Remove from the oven and let cool before serving. Cover the pie with aluminum foil and store in the refrigerator or an ice-filled cooler for up to 48 hours. Be careful not to put anything on top of it.

Apple Brown Betty

Whoever the Betty was that came up with this dish, I want to thank her. Frankly, while I don't hate making piecrusts, like Melville's *Bartleby*, I'd prefer not to.

Here you can use leftover bread, biscuits, or even pound cake. And though you have to brown it in the oven, it's a lot easier than rolling out dough for a crust.

SERVES 8

6 medium apples // 1/2 lemon // 4 cups cubed day-old bread, biscuits, or cake // 1/2 cup (1 stick) cold butter // 1/2 cup packed brown sugar // 1 teaspoon cinnamon // 1/4 teaspoon ground nutmeg, preferably freshly grated // Pinch cloves // Vanilla ice cream for serving

1. Preheat the oven to 300°F.

2. Peel and core the apples and cut them into 3/4-inch slices. Transfer to a large bowl, squeeze the lemon over the apple slices and toss gently to cover the apples and keep them from browning before baking. Set aside.

3. On a 12-by-17-inch baking sheet, arrange the bread or biscuit cubes in one layer and bake on the center rack of the oven until lightly brown, about 10 minutes.

4. Meanwhile, melt the butter in a small saucepan. When the bread cubes are done, transfer them to a large bowl, pour on half of the melted butter, and toss together. Set aside.

5. Add the sugar, cinnamon, nutmeg, and cloves to the apples and gently toss together.

6. Raise the oven temperature to 375°F.

7. Place one third of the toasted bread cubes on the bottom of a 9-inch square baking pan. Top with half of the apple slices. Top with another one third of the bread cubes and then the remaining apples. Top the apples with the remaining bread cubes. Pour the remaining butter over everything.

8. Bake on the center rack for 30 minutes, until the top is nicely browned.

9. Remove from heat and serve warm with vanilla ice cream.

10. Brown Betty is best made the same day you are going to serve it as once you cover and store it, it loses its consistency.

8
Drinks

I like to welcome friends to a meal with some kind of interesting and pleasing cocktail. It's not the alcohol that's important. It's the idea that you are sharing a meal together and the drink marks the beginning of that event.

When the drink has a surprising flavor, it also ensures that the meal starts out on a happy note.

Tailgating celebrations include drinks of all kinds. It makes singing around the campfire and expressing your unconditional devotion to your favorite driver that much more fun. But be sure to be attentive to some of these drinks. Their easy, golden taste belies their kick.

Watermelon Gin and Tonic

The color and unexpected flavor of this drink make it a must for a hot summer day. You can make the watermelon juice in advance; just keep it cold in a refrigerator or ice-filled cooler for up to 3 days.

MAKES 4 DRINKS

1 ripe whole watermelon to yield 8 ounces fresh watermelon juice (see recipe method) // 8 ounces gin // 8 ounces tonic // Ice // Fresh mint for garnish

1. **TO MAKE THE WATERMELON JUICE:** Cut the watermelon into thick slices and remove the rind and whitish parts. Place the watermelon in a food processor fitted with the metal blade and zap to a smooth, slushy texture. Pour into a large pitcher and allow the seeds to settle to the bottom. *Voilà!* This is watermelon juice.

2. **TO MAKE THE GIN AND TONIC:** Stir the watermelon juice and gin together over ice into four tall glasses. Add the tonic gingerly and garnish with the fresh mint.

Negroni

The *negroni* is one of the great Italian cocktails. Salvador Dali and Luis Bunuel concocted this legendary cocktail on the set of their infamous film *Un Chien Andalou.*

MAKES 3 DRINKS

5 ounces dry gin // 5 ounces campari // 5 ounces sweet vermouth // Ice // Orange twists

1. In a large cocktail shaker, combine the gin, campari, and vermouth. Shake gently.
2. Pour over ice into a large balloon glass.
3. Twist the orange peel to release the juices, drop the peels into the cocktail and serve.

Raspberry Rum Punch

Here's a sprightly summer drink, pretty to look at and with a deviously delicious taste.

MAKES 8 DRINKS

Ice cubes // 24 ounces club soda or raspberry-flavored seltzer // 1 cup freshly squeezed orange juice (about 4 oranges) // 8 ounces rum // 8 ounces Amaretto // 1 cup fresh or frozen raspberries, pureed // 1 orange, thinly sliced // Mint sprigs

I. Put the ice cubes in a punch bowl.

2. Add the remaining ingredients.

3. Stir lightly and serve immediately.

Strawberry Lemonade

You will want to be attentive to the kids getting a hold of this drink, only because they are liable to finish it in one sitting.

MAKES 1 QUART

1 pint fresh strawberries, hulled and halved, plus more whole strawberries for garnish // 1 cup sugar // 1 cup water // 1 tablespoon grated lemon peel // 1 cup freshly squeezed lemon juice (about 8 lemons) // 2 cups cold sparkling water or club soda // Ice // Mint sprigs for garnish

I. In a blender or food processor fitted with the metal blade, puree the pint of strawberries with the sugar, then add the water and zap again.

2. Pour the mixture into a large pitcher along with the grated lemon peel and lemon juice and chill well.

3. When ready to serve, slowly add the club soda and top off the pitcher with ice. Stir well, pour into tall glasses, and serve garnished with the mint and some strawberries.

Mint Juleps

You don't have be a Southern belle sitting on your front porch rocker trying to remember the Minuet to enjoy these classic summer drinks.

MAKES 8 DRINKS

9 lemons // 2 cups sugar // 1½ cups water // 24 mint sprigs // Ice // 3 cups bourbon

1. Squeeze 8 of the lemons into a small saucepan. Add 1¼ cups of the sugar, the water, and 5 or 6 of the lemon rinds and bring the liquid to a boil. Reduce the heat to medium and simmer until the mixture thickens, about 12 minutes. Let cool.

2. Put the remaining sugar in a small bowl or cereal bowl. Quarter the remaining lemon and rub the top of 8 tall tumblers with it. Press the tops of the glasses into the sugar to coat.

3. Place 2 mint sprigs in each glass and crush them with a wooden spoon. Fill each glass with ice, then with the lemon syrup. Add 2 to 4 ounces of bourbon to each glass, depending on how strong each guest likes his or her drink. Garnish with the remaining sprigs of mint and serve.

Happy Hour Watermelon

If your spouse has ever accused you of being neither creative nor industrious, you can take out those potholders you made in summer camp or you can demonstrate both talents by assembling this drink concoction.

MAKES 20 DRINKS

1 fifth vodka // 1 ripe whole watermelon

1. Cut a 2-by-2-inch hole in the top of the melon, wide and deep enough to insert a (clean) funnel. Pour half of the bottle of vodka into the melon through the funnel, replace the plug, then refrigerate or store in an ice-filled cooler for 24 hours. (Make sure it's propped up so it doesn't tip.)

2. The next day, pour in as much of the remaining vodka as you can. The melon flesh will absorb the liquid until it becomes saturated. Keep cold in a refrigerator or ice-filled cooler until ready to serve.

3. When ready to eat/drink, slice the watermelon into large pieces and serve.

NOTE: For obvious reasons, buy the kids their own watermelon.

Horchata

An *horchata* is a traditional Mexican drink. Try bringing along a pitcher if you're visiting some new tailgating friends. The *horchata's* surprising flavor and curious ingredients will make for a great conversation starter.

SERVES 8 TO 10

1½ cups long grain white rice // 2 cups sliced blanched almonds // 2 tablespoons cinnamon //
2½ cups sugar // Ice // 1 bunch fresh mint for garnish

1. Rinse the rice. Put in a bowl or pan with water to cover and soak overnight. Drain well.

2. Put the rice, almonds, and cinnamon in a blender or food processor fitted with the metal blade. Add 2 cups cold water and zap until the mixture turns to paste (basically, the texture of mud).

3. Mix the rice/almond paste, sugar, and 3 quarts of water in a large glass jar or clear pitcher and stir well. Refrigerate to chill.

4. Serve the *horchata* in tall glasses over ice cubes garnished with mint leaves.

NOTE: You can enhance this drink by adding some dark rum.

Track Information

ATLANTA MOTOR SPEEDWAY

Opened: 1960
Owner: Speedway Motorsports, Inc.
Location: Hampton, Ga.
Distance: 1.54 miles
Banking in turns: 24 degrees
Banking in straights: 5 degrees
Length of front stretch: 2,332 feet
Length of back stretch: 1,800 feet
Tickets: (770) 946-4211
Website: atlantamotorspeedway.com

BRISTOL MOTOR SPEEDWAY

Opened: 1961
Owner: Speedway Motorsports, Inc.
Location: Bristol, Tenn.
Distance: .533 miles
Banking in turns: 36 degrees
Banking in straights: 16 degrees
Length of front stretch: 650 feet
Length of back stretch: 650 feet
Tickets: (423) 764-1161
Website: bristolmotorspeedway.com

CALIFORNIA SPEEDWAY

Opened: 1997
Owner: International Speedway Corp.
Location: Fontana, Calif.
Distance: 2.0 miles
Banking in Turns 1-4: 14 degrees
Banking in trioval: 11 degrees
Banking in back stretch: 3 degrees
Length of front stretch: 3,100 feet
Length of back stretch: 2,500 feet
Tickets: (800) 944-7223
Website: californiaspeedway.com

CHICAGOLAND SPEEDWAY

Opened: 2001
Owner: Raceway Associates, LLC
Location: Joliet, Ill.
Distance: 1.5 miles
Banking in turns: 18 degrees
Banking in trioval: 11 degrees
Banking in back stretch: 5 degrees
Length of front stretch: 2,400 feet
Length of back stretch: 1,700 feet
Tickets: (815) 727-7223
Website: chicagolandspeedway.com

DARLINGTON RACEWAY

Opened: 1950
Owner: International Speedway Corp.
Location: Darlington, S.C.
Distance: 1.366 miles
Banking in Turns 1-2: 25 degrees
Banking in Turns 3-4: 23 degrees
Banking in front stretch: 3 degrees
Banking in back stretch: 2 degrees
Length of front stretch: 1,229 feet
Length of back stretch: 1,229 feet
Tickets: (843) 395-8499
Website: darlingtonraceway.com

DAYTONA INTERNATIONAL SPEEDWAY

Opened: 1959
Owner: International Speedway Corp.
Location: Daytona Beach, Fla.
Distance: 2.5 miles
Banking in turns: 31 degrees
Banking in trioval: 18 degrees
Banking in back stretch: 3 degrees
Length of front stretch: 3,800 feet

Length of back stretch: 3,000 feet
Tickets: (386) 253-7223
Website: daytonainternationalspeedway.com

DOVER INTERNATIONAL SPEEDWAY

Opened: 1969
Owner: Dover Downs Entertainment Inc.
Location: Dover, Del.
Distance: 1 mile
Banking in turns: 24 degrees
Banking in straights: 9 degrees
Length of front stretch: 1,076 feet
Length of back stretch: 1,076 feet
Tickets: (800) 441-7223
Website: www.doverspeedway.com

HOMESTEAD-MIAMI SPEEDWAY

Opened: 1995
Owner: International Speedway Corp.
Location: Homestead, Fla.
Distance: 1.5 miles
Banking in turns: Variable,
18 to 20 degrees
Banking in straights: 4 degrees
Length of front stretch: 1,760 feet
Length of back stretch: 1,760 feet
Tickets: (305) 230-7223
Website: www.homesteadmiamispeedway.com

INDIANAPOLIS MOTOR SPEEDWAY

Opened: 1909
Owner: Hulman-George Family, Hulman & Co.
Location: Indianapolis, Ind.
Distance: 2.5 miles
Banking in turns: 9 degrees, 12 minutes
Banking in straights: 0 degrees
Length of font stretch: 3,300 feet
Length of back stretch: 3,300 feet
Length of short straightaways: 660 feet

Tickets: (317) 481-6700
Website: www.brickyard400.com

INFINEON RACEWAY

Opened: 1968
Owner: Speedway Motorsports, Inc.
Location: Sonoma, Calif.
Distance: 1.99-mile road course
Turns: 11, with varying lengths and degrees of banking.
The chute: 890 feet, 2.8 degrees of banking
Tickets: (800) 870-7223
Website: www.infineonraceway.com

KANSAS SPEEDWAY

Opened: 2001
Owner: International Speedway Corp.
Location: Kansas City, Kan.
Distance: 1.5 miles
Banking in turns: 15 degrees
Banking in front stretch: 10.4 degrees
Banking in back stretch: 5 degrees
Length of front stretch: 2,685 feet
Length of back stretch: 2,207 feet
Tickets: (913) 328-7223
Website: www.kansasspeedway.com

LAS VEGAS MOTOR SPEEDWAY

Opened: 1996
Owner: Speedway Motorsports, Inc.
Location: Las Vegas, Nev.
Distance: 1.5 miles
Banking in turns: 12 degrees
Banking in front stretch: 9 degrees
Banking in back stretch: 3 degrees
Length of front stretch: 2.275 feet
Length of back stretch: 1,572 feet
Tickets: (702) 644-4444
Website: www.lvms.com

LOWE'S MOTOR SPEEDWAY

Opened: 1960
Owner: Speedway Motorsports, Inc.
Location: Concord, N.C.
Distance: 1.5-mile oval
Banking in turns: 24 degrees
Banking in straights: 5 degrees
Length of front stretch: 1,952 feet
Length of back stretch: 1,360 feet
Tickets: (704) 455-3267
Website: www.lowesmotorspeedway.com

MARTINSVILLE SPEEDWAY

Opened: 1947
Owner: International Speedway Corp.
Location: Martinsville, Va.
Distance: .526 miles
Banking in turns: 12 degrees
Banking in straights: None
Length of front stretch: 800 feet
Length of back stretch: 800 feet
Tickets: (276) 956-3151 or (877) 722-3849
Website: www.martinsvillespeedway.com

MICHIGAN INTERNATIONAL SPEEDWAY

Opened: 1968
Owner: International Speedway Corp.
Location: Brooklyn, Mich.
Distance: 2 miles
Banking in turns: 18 degrees
Banking in front stretch: 12 degrees
Banking in back stretch: 5 degrees
Length of front stretch: 3,600 feet
Length of back stretch: 2,242 feet
Tickets: (800) 354-1010
Website: www.mispeedway.com

NEW HAMPSHIRE INTERNATIONAL SPEEDWAY

Opened: 1990

Owner: Bob Bahre
Location: Loudon, N.H.
Distance: 1.058 miles
Banking in turns: 12 degrees
Banking in straights: 2 degrees
Length of front stretch: 1,500 feet
Length of back stretch: 1,500 feet
Tickets: (603) 783-4931
Website: www.nhis.com

PHOENIX INTERNATIONAL RACEWAY

Opened: 1964
Owner: International Speedway Corp.
Location: Avondale, Ariz.
Distance: 1 mile
Banking in Turns 1-2: 11 degrees
Banking in Turns 3-4: 9 degrees
Banking in straights: None
Length of front stretch: 1,179 feet
Length of back stretch: 1,551 feet
Tickets: (602) 252-2227
Website: www.phoenixintlraceway.com

POCONO RACEWAY

Date Opened: 1968
Owner: Pocono Raceway, Inc.
Location: Long Pond, Pa.
Distance: 2.5 miles
Banking in Turn 1: 14 degrees
Banking in Turn 2: 8 degrees
Banking in Turn 3: 6 degrees
Length of front stretch: 3,740 feet
Length of short stretch: 1,780 feet
Length of back stretch: 3,055 feet
Tickets: (800) 722-3939
Website: www.poconoraceway.com

RICHMOND INTERNATIONAL RACEWAY

Date opened: 1946

Owner: International Speedway Corp.

Location: Richmond, Va.

Distance: .750 miles

Banking in turns: 14 degrees

Banking on front stretch: 8 degrees

Banking on back stretch: 2 degrees

Length of front stretch: 1,290 feet

Length of back stretch: 860 feet

Tickets: (804) 345-7223

Website: www.rir.com

TALLADEGA SUPERSPEEDWAY

Opened: 1969

Owner: International Speedway Corp.

Location: Talladega, Ala.

Distance: 2.66 miles

Banking in turns: 33 degrees

Banking in trioval: 18 degrees

Banking on back stretch: 2 degrees

Length of front stretch: 4,300 feet

Length of backstretch: 4,000 feet

Tickets: (256) 362-7223

Website: www.talladegasuperspeedway.com

TEXAS MOTOR SPEEDWAY

Date Opened: 1996

Owner: Speedway Motorsports, Inc.

Location: Fort Worth, Texas

Distance: 1.5 miles

Banking in turns: 24 degrees

Banking in straights: 5 degrees

Length of front stretch: 2,250 feet

Length of back stretch: 1,330 feet

Tickets: (817) 215-8500

Website: www.texasmotorspeedway.com

WATKINS GLEN INTERNATIONAL

Date Opened: 1956

Owner: International Speedway Corp.

Location: Watkins Glen, N.Y.

Distance: 2.45-mile road course

Turns: 11

Banking: Ranging from 6 to 10 degrees

Pit road stretch: 2,141 feet

Length of back stretch: 1,839 feet

Tickets: (607) 535-2481

Website: www.theglen.com

Index

For more information on **2 BROTHERS** Barbecue Sauce, go to: www.2brothersbrand.com.